D1360348

MANARIN
On MONEY

MANARIN

On MONEY

A Real World Guide to Building and Maintaining Wealth

by Roland R. Manarin

WINANS
KUENSTLER
PUBLISHING LLC

Published in the United States by
Winans Kuenstler Publishing
www.WKPublishing.com

To order additional copies and for more information:
www.ManarinOnMoney.com
The author may be contacted at:
Manarin Investment Counsel
15858 West Dodge Road Suite 310
Omaha, Nebraska 68118
(800) 397-1167
investor@manarin.com
www.manarin.com

First Edition
Printed in the United States of America

Contents

Dedication

A very special thank you to my Papa who left his home and country to emigrate to a new continent in search of a better life and opportunities for his family.

A very special thank you to my Mama for her undying love and support.

MANARIN ON MONEY

Introduction

THE VOLUME you hold in your hands is the distillation of a lifetime of experience studying how money works, including a quarter century of observing how the investment industry routinely fails to deliver on its promises. What I've learned could fill a book, so I did.

My first peek inside the financial services business came soon after graduating from the University of Nebraska at Omaha in the 1960s, when I took a job selling life insurance. I had no expertise in financial investments but I did know something about the value of a dollar. I had been working steadily since I was fifteen, when I started out as a stock boy in a grocery store, rising up the ladder over a number of years to become second assistant manager.

I had worked my way through college. At 16, when I bought my first "beater" used car for $40, I parked it a block away from home because I didn't want my father to know I had made such a recklessly indulgent purchase.

In my family, money symbolized more than freedom—it was survival. When I was an infant, my parents and other relatives spent World War II dodging the war in Germany—and then fleeing back to our home in the foothills of the Italian alps. Our struggle continued after the war, coping with a shattered economy and then the Soviet Army, which rolled into the German city of Breslau (now located in Poland) and confiscated my family's prosperous marble-fabrication business. We lost everything. At least they didn't send us Italians to the gulags like they did the Germans.

As did so many other European refugees, we ended up following my father to the United States, to Omaha, Nebraska. In his case, an American contractor visiting Italy had met and hired him to go work on building projects. My father was a master European craftsman from the uncompromising old school. He took great pride in his craft and did well enough to bring the rest of us over in April of 1954.

I was ten at the time, and entered my teen years living the charmed life of an American kid but with an acute and ever-present awareness of just how cruel and unpredictable the future can be. No one had to tell me how important it was to have the financial flexibility to survive life's inevitable bouts of stormy weather.

Early in my short career selling life insurance, my manager sent me out to visit a family that had responded to a marketing solicitation. The manager explained that the policy he wanted me to sell them paid $5,000 if any member of the family died, including the children.

I arrived at the home to discover they had five kids and one breadwinner—the father. My boss's instructions made no sense. If the father died first, the mother and all those kids would burn through that $5,000—equal in buying power to about $30,000 in 2007—in no time. Then what?

I sat down at their kitchen table, and began by showing the couple the plan my boss had instructed me to talk them into buying. Shuffling through my materials, I turned to the father and said, "But if the person who dies is the breadwinner, the money won't keep your family going very long. For the same premium, you can get a policy that pays $50,000 if you die, instead of $5,000 if, God forbid, somebody else does."

The choice was as clear to them as it was to me, and they showed their appreciation for my thoughtfulness and honesty by buying the better policy.

The next morning, I walked into the office filled with a sense of achievement. I'd made a sale and done a good deed. I had given that father and mother peace of mind, and saved the family from what could have been a financial disaster. But instead of a pat on the back, I got a slap in the face.

"What's the big idea!" my boss blurted when I handed him the paperwork. "This isn't the policy I told you to sell. It's the wrong one!"

"What do you mean? What's wrong with it?" I panicked, thinking I'd really messed something up for those people.

"Heck, we hardly make any commission on the policy you sold. That was a solid lead, Roland, and you blew a good commission for us. This is a business, not a charity! You're supposed to sell what makes us the most money."

It was all I could do to maintain my composure. I was stunned at his callousness, shocked that I was expected to knowingly put the financial security of others in jeopardy so we could make a few extra commission dollars. I was disgusted, swore at him in Italian, and quit.

That was the moment the seed was planted that would later sprout and grow into a philosophy about money and investment that has made me a relatively wealthy, contented person who sleeps well. I have helped thousands avoid disaster and achieve financial independence, however they defined it. Along the way I have witnessed both the foolishness and wisdom of others.

I have watched up close the devastation that comes from believing in the "sure thing." The collapse of Enron was keenly felt in Omaha, where the company had a large office, and there are today quite a few ex-millionaires in our community who, instead of enjoying a comfortable retirement, are hand-cuffed to low-paying service jobs to make ends meet.

I have also witnessed the extraordinary investment success of another of our locals, Warren Buffett, who became one of the wealthiest men in the world by relying on common sense.

Along the way I learned that the industry that says it wants to help you grow wealthy and stay that way is actually just a marketing machine, intent on selling you products designed to line its pockets first, and yours only by coincidence. It was a long time ago that my boss tried to get me to foist a bad choice on the unsuspecting, but little has changed, except the terminology and the technology.

It would be some years after I quit the insurance company that I committed my fulltime career to being an investment professional. For the past three decades, I have devoted my life to helping people resist the temptations of the *sure thing*. But that's not enough by itself to grow and preserve wealth. Financial independence can't be found in a bank CD or treasury bond, let alone a mattress.

As you'll read in the following pages, I learned how to grow wealth by studying the rules and using them to win instead of sell. I've watched how others squandered it, not just on sure things, but by entrusting their financial lives to people who didn't believe in, and often didn't understand, the investment "products" they were selling.

Early on, I broke away from that crowd to chart my own path, believing in the principle that if I did the right thing for my clients, it would end up the right thing for me as well. As a result, I have been successful mainly because I helped my clients become successful.

How this all happened, and how I developed the principles that have guided my investment philosophy and achievement, has been a journey of discovery that I invite you to share and profit from, just as I did. In these pages, you will learn how money works, and how you can make it work for you, instead of the other way around.

"Money," says an old proverb, "is a good servant and a bad master." In a culture obsessed with striking it rich—awash with competing, conflicting, confusing, and mostly useless investment advice—you may be surprised to find that certain basic rules about growing and protecting money have not changed, and never will.

I encourage you to turn off the financial news channel on television, ignore the prognostications you hear about and read in the media, quit buying books about how to get rich quick, toss in the trash all the junk mail you get from investment companies, avoid discussing investments on golf courses and at dinner parties, and spend a few hours with me on a quiet journey to a world of calm and common sense. Something in these pages could change your life by helping you make a good choice or avoid a bad one, steering you away from struggle and anxiety, and toward security and independence.

—ROLAND R. MANARIN
Omaha, Nebraska, 2008

PART I:

The Truth About Money

1

Mr. College Smart-Guy

AMERICANS ARE, on average, the richest people in the world. Yet we are also the most irresponsible and befuddled when it comes to taking care of our wealth, whether it's a weekly paycheck or a big inheritance. We have frittered away our home equity on boats and vacations. We spend everything we earn, and then borrow more. We chase hot tips. We gamble.

> **The road to success is not doing one thing 100 percent better... but doing one hundred things one percent better.**
>
> —H. Jackson Brown, Jr., author of "Life's Little Instruction Book"

We hand over our money to total strangers because their shoes are shined and their linen-paper business cards say they are experts in investments. After all, there's always tomorrow.

But you know all that. It's why you're reading this book. You know something's wrong. Something doesn't make sense. Something's not adding up.

You may be worried about growing old in poverty. You may have financial goals that, the harder you try to reach them, the further away they seem to recede. Maybe you were burned during the meltdown that followed the 1990s stock market bubble. Maybe you chased the real estate craze and now you're stuck with mortgage payments on an empty investment condo in Florida. Maybe you're tired of reading about cheating on Wall Street and watching your investments limp along while the brokerage houses who handle your money grow obscenely fat.

Maybe you're just so confused by all the hype and hoopla, you've stuck your money in the modern equivalent of a mattress—a bank CD—where it slowly and steadily loses buying power to the relentless force of inflation.

Whatever it is that's making you uneasy, you want the truth and you want to know in plain English what it takes to build and protect your wealth. That's why I decided it was time to put down in one place—after years of lecturing and broadcasting about it—the inside story of how the investment business really works, how you can avoid common traps and pitfalls that rob you of wealth opportunities, and how you can take control of your financial future without needing a degree in economics or the predatory instincts of a jackal.

My Old World Lessons

Americans lack a fundamental understanding of how money works. Our parents, our educational system, and the financial industry have proven themselves incapable of teaching the basics that you are about to learn in these pages. Many of these lessons are

> **Once you understand how money works and grows, you have the tools to create financial independence.**

rooted in monetary history. Once you understand how money works and how it grows, you have the tools to create financial independence, which in turn will give you a kind of peace of mind that very few Americans enjoy.

Luck and brilliance have little or nothing to do with the ability to have success. It's simply time, discipline, and the knowledge of what money must do to achieve your goals. I know, because I learned it the hard way. My "higher" education in money began in 1976.

"Okay Mr. College Smart-Guy. What should I do with my money?"

The question was posed to me by my first and most important investment client. I was thirty-two years old, beginning my career as a stockbroker, working for one of the leading brokerage firms.

Twenty-two years earlier, I'd stepped off a boat in New York harbor, a ten-year-old immigrant from northern Italy on my way to America's heartland, knowing how to speak Italian, Friulian (spoken in northeastern Italy), and German, but no English. Like another, more famous, American, I was born in a log cabin, except this one was in the mountains of modern day Czech Republic. Back then the region was occupied by Nazi Germany. My mother was German, my father Italian. So our family had retreated to the mountains to ride out the war.

I was less than a year old when the war ended in 1945. My family's prosperous business had been in Breslau, Germany.

They ended up stuck behind the Iron Curtain of Communism. Soviet troops rolled in and confiscated all their assets.

So my father loaded us all onto a cattle car headed to the small village of Fanna in northern Italy, where we settled down in the house of my father's family and I got my early education. We had survived Europe's conflagration, but times remained lean in the immediate post-war years as the battered economies struggled to recover.

Like so many other displaced Europeans, my father found a solution to our problem in America. One day an American contractor showed up in our village asking to meet some marble workers. My father had a good reputation so it wasn't long before the two met. The man said there was a lot of work in a place called Omaha, a building boom, and not enough skilled craftsmen to keep up with demand. He wanted to hire my father to go to Omaha and practice his profession.

This was a similar path taken by my grandfather, who shoveled coal on a steamer in the 1890s to work his way to America. He found work on the east coast, including laying mosaics, some of which can still be seen in older buildings. When he'd saved up a nest egg, he returned to Italy and started his own business doing marble work for the dukes and barons in Germany. He became very successful.

Now it was my father's turn to find opportunity abroad. With much weeping and hope, we walked him down to the railroad depot one day in 1952 and sent him on his way across the ocean to the land of cowboys and Indians—the steppes of North America—and the golden promise of peace and prosperity.

After two years of sending money home, my father had saved enough to send for the rest of us. We, too, made the walk to the train station with much weeping and hope, bidding goodbye to our relatives who were staying behind, but anxious to see the wonderful things Papa had been writing us about all those months.

I had learned a lot in my first thirty or so years of life, but I was hardly qualified to be blithely handing out investment advice.

New World Lessons

I quickly overcame the language barrier as the kids in my new neighborhood in Omaha were kind enough to teach me a few key words that gave me a leg up for my studies in grade school. It also helped that I was ahead of the other kids in math, thanks to the emphasis in my classes in Italy on numbers, calculations, and figures. In high school I took as many college-level math courses as I could find. At the University of Nebraska-Omaha I earned my degree in business administration.

I had tried selling life insurance early, then spent several years selling office equipment (typewriters, word processors, and so on), after which I sold forms through systems analysis. A few years later, through a friend, I found myself drawn into the business of stock brokerage. I had learned a lot in my first thirty or so years of life, but I was hardly qualified to be blithely handing out investment advice.

Trying to conceal my panic of self-doubt, I faced my first real client, racking my brain for an intelligent answer.

"Well, Mr. College Smart-Guy? What should I do?" The 73-year-old man drummed his thick, muscular fingers on my desk and gazed into my eyes. I nervously doodled with my new company pen on my new company scratch pad, and cleared my throat. I was supposed to sell him something, make a commission for my company and myself. But I'm a terrible liar so I threw myself on the mercy of the court.

"I don't know. But I'm going to figure it out, Papa. As soon as I do, I'll let you know."

I've had tougher clients than my father in the past thirty-odd years, but none of them had made the sacrifices he did on my behalf. Every cent in his pocket was serious money, and I felt it in my bones. Thus, I began my career in the business of helping people grow their money with a tremendous sense of responsibility. In time, I came to understand that for most people, all money is serious money, and every client deserves an honest answer.

I was introduced to the investment industry in the 1970s by a close friend named Ron who had been pestering me for years to get into the business. In 1973 I agreed to go for an interview with a brokerage firm in Minneapolis. I hated it. The guy who interviewed me bragged that he had a Masters degree in psychology, and that he was an ex-professional football player. He was a narcissist, self-important, and condescending. I told him I'd grown up poor, thinking this was a selling point—I understood the value of a dollar. Instead he replied, "You can't think small in this business. You gotta think big. That's something maybe you should think about. Can you think big enough to make it? 'Cause if you can't, don't waste my time."

I returned to Omaha and told Ron, "They could offer me three times what I'm earning now and I still wouldn't work for those blankety-blanks."

A few years later, Ron had moved up the ladder and become the branch manager of a different brokerage firm. He liked his company and told me that it wasn't like the other brokerage firms. "They really aren't taking advantage of the customers. They don't force you to sell things people don't need. They think more like you do, Roland. Customers are number one."

He whispered sweet nothings in my ear until I succumbed. Once snared by the idea, I looked forward to the experience. As long as I was helping people build and maintain wealth, it seemed like a worthwhile vocation. And maybe I could figure out how to become wealthy myself.

> This was a surprise—stock brokers who know nothing about the fundamentals of building and maintaining wealth.

Life As a Rookie

Nine months on the job and I wasn't so sure. Life as a rookie broker was difficult. After a short period of training, focused mainly on brokerage rules, procedures, and sales, I was pointed toward a desk, a chair, and a telephone, and instructed to bring in new clients. Concerned, I asked Ron, "Is this it for training? Is this all they're going to teach me about investing?"

"Yes," he proudly said. "It's the best training program in the country."

"Based on what you guys have taught me, I'm not going to invest what little my father saved," I replied.

Ron smiled. "Roland, with your background and knowledge, you know more than all the other brokers here and that's about all you'll need in this business to get started."

This was a surprise—stock brokers who know nothing about the fundamentals of building and maintaining wealth.

There was no way I was going to invest my parents' lifetime savings based on their ignorance.

It would have been easy to listen to the brokerage firm, sell the products they told me to, earn my commissions, and go home fat and happy. But I had a different take on things. Now I had a challenge, to figure out what the real deal was.

From that point on, much of my private time was devoted to studying and teaching myself about money so that I would someday be able to give my father an answer to his question that I knew to be true. So Mr. College Smart Guy went back to work—absorbing as much knowledge as I could about money and how it grows.

Up until that time, my investing experience was probably quite typical. Through Ron, I bought a stock here and another one there. One would gain fifty percent and I thought I was a genius. The other would lose fifty percent and I thought I was a fool. In the end the only money was made by the brokerage firm. Even my friend Ron had no clue. In fact, as I grew better educated, I began to teach him a few things. Up until that point, he was no different from a vacuum cleaner salesman. He had a product line and his job was to sell it.

It would have been easy to listen to the brokerage firm, sell the products they told me to, earn my commissions, and go home fat and happy. But I had a different take on things.

My father's question, what to do with his money, was a challenge but it was also an opportunity to prove myself. He was completely supportive and went to the trouble of having a case of match books custom printed with my name on them, to hand out like business cards. When he asked me for advice, I told him the truth: I have no idea, but as soon as I figure it out, you'll be the first to know.

After about six months of studying up on money and investing, the more I learned the more I realized how little I knew, and the more I felt I probably shouldn't be handling other people's money. One day, after a particularly guilt-ridden and frustrating night, I arrived at the office and told Ron, "This is no good. I'm not making any money because I'm not sure enough to make suggestions and give advice. I think I should just quit and chalk it up to experience."

"No, no, no!" he insisted. "Don't worry about the money for now. I'll make sure you're earning enough to get by until things click. It takes time, is all. Listen, we need more people like you who are honest. You've got more integrity and insight in your left pinky finger than most of the other guys in our industry. You understand the money game better than you realize."

So Ron talked me into continuing my studies.

My First Breakthrough

Later on, I had impressed Ron by uncovering an opportunity that seemed to me like money laying on the ground just waiting for someone to come along and pick it up. I stumbled across an equity mutual fund that was internationally diversified and well-managed. The portfolio manager held stocks for an average of three to five years instead of a few months.

The average rate of return for this fund ranged between 12 and 14 percent in typical yo-yo fashion. The more I looked into it the more annoyed I became that nobody ever taught me about such funds. But I was glad, too. I'd found something good for Papa.

Our brokerage firm, along with the rest of industry, pushed clients to buy individual stocks, bonds, mutual funds and unit trusts. My firm, like the others, had its recommended buy/sell list. When I came across this fund on my own, I called up the head of our mutual fund department and asked him if he had heard of it.

"Who?" he asked. Here was the best fund I had ever seen—a mutual fund I still own today—and the so-called experts hadn't even heard of it. I poked around and found a few others like it that had good long-term records with low risk.

This turned me into a pain in the behind in the office. I began to ask embarrassing questions: Why are we selling stocks and bonds when these diversified funds have done so well, virtually their entire existence? The answer turned out to be the same one I got when I sold that family a $50,000 term insurance policy instead of the one I'd been instructed to sell. Commissions were higher on individual stocks and bonds because there was more trading involved.

I did all my research on my own, no help from my company, because the higher-ups only wanted to do business with funds that did business with them. A mutual fund buys and sells stocks just like individuals and our brokerage firm only wanted to push funds managed by companies that used our trading desk to make its buys and sells. Thus, the firm had a clear conflict of interest. They were getting paid off, in a sense, for pushing certain funds because those funds were buying our trad-

> I began to ask embarrassing questions: Why are we selling stocks and bonds when these diversified funds have done so well, virtually their entire existence?

ing services, on which the company made commissions. This fact was never disclosed to clients, of course.

Before I took the plunge, I sat down with Ron and showed him the fund I discovered and its solid, long-term rate of return. "Okay, nice fund. So what?"

"Now, think about this," I said. "We've got a lot of equity in our homes, and your house is almost paid off, right? If you took out a new first mortgage, you'd have cash to invest that cost you about 4 to 5 percent after the tax break on interest payments. If we put that money into this fund and cross our arms, we win!"

Ron looked at the performance chart, stroked his chin, and looked at me with a light-bulb expression. "Gosh, Roland. I think you're right."

"I'm the rookie here," I said. "How come I have to tell you this?"

"I told you before," Ron said. "You're a natural."

So we both pulled equity out of our houses and plunked it down on the fund and from that point on, I showed Ron how to go beyond being just a salesman and really teach people how to build and maintain wealth. From then on, he let me make my own choices for clients and didn't pressure me to sell high-commission products. I was happy, and my clients were doing well.

> Ron stroked his chin, and looked at me with a light-bulb expression. "Gosh, Roland. I think you're right."
> "I'm the rookie here," I said. "How come I have to tell you this?"

A Look At the Dark Side

Now that I had my good idea, I put Papa's savings into the same mutual fund and a few others, including some funds that invested in gold-mining stocks. That was my hedge against disaster, something I knew about personally. When World War II ended and my family fled the Soviet-controlled part of Germany to our home in Italy, my parents carried what they could salvage of their money in gold, hidden under my diapers.

The gold hedge occurred to me in the second half of the 1970s when the Carter administration's policies were, in my view, setting the stage for more inflation, not less. Gold is a hedge against inflation, monetary crisis, and international instability. As we saw in 2007, gold rises during periods of economic uncertainty. But I knew from my studies that buying the metal to protect a portfolio was not the way to go, other than keeping a few gold coins at home as an emergency stash.

The best way to hedge an investment portfolio using gold is to buy shares of a mutual fund that invests exclusively in gold-mining companies. When the price of gold rises above the cost of production, the mutual fund shares will tend to rise at a faster pace than the metal itself.

My new boss made it clear up front that I was expected to push the products he wanted me to sell, not what I thought was best for my customers.

In my fourth year with the company, my friend Ron keeled over one day and died of a heart attack, at the age of 38. It was a personal shock, followed by a professional one. His replacement as the office manager turned out to be just like the arrogant guy in Minneapolis who had turned me off so many years before. He made it clear up front that I was expected to push the products he wanted me to sell, not what I thought was best for my customers.

As callous as my insurance company boss had been, this guy was even worse. He bragged about "churning" his own mother's account. Churning is the unethical and illegal practice of buying and selling stocks and bonds for clients simply to generate commissions. In our staff meetings, he'd crow about having made a $1000 commission off his mother's account. It was disgusting.

I don't mean to tar the entire industry with this brush. There are many ethical, caring investment advisors in our business. But most are unable to connect the dots so they are unable to see the whole story and therefore unable to give their clients the best-possible advice.

Later, my new boss and I ended up going head to head when a customer of his attended a seminar I gave and asked me what to do with his money. I told him to put it into the conservative mutual funds that I was using for myself and my clients. He did, and a year or two later he was about 30 percent richer.

But then my boss convinced him to sell the funds and buy a motley collection of other investments that I knew generated fatter commissions. I was furious and complained to the president of the firm, to his face, at a company meeting. The president's response? He ordered the branch manager to fire me. I was a trouble-maker. But the branch manager balked. I was one of his top brokers and making a lot of money, of which he got a cut as branch manager. Firing me would reduce his income.

Declaring My Independence

By the summer of 1982, I had about $18 million of other people's money under management, a large sum for an individual broker at the time. I was in the top one percent of the firm's brokers, with the best office in the place. That August, I got a visit from the regional manager and the branch manager. The regional manager was a classic stock trader who barely understood what a mutual fund was.

They started off by congratulating me on my success. Then they breathlessly told me about an exciting new trading program the company was rolling out.

"Roland, as good as you are, if you put half the money you manage in on this new trading program you'll triple your commissions. You'll make a fortune, with all the money you manage. Just think of it!"

My ears began to burn. It sounded like a scam, a way of getting people to make bad choices so we could take more of their money. I took a deep breath, counted to ten and, as calmly as I could manage, told them the new program didn't sound right for most of my clients, but (I lied) I would look into it. I left the office that day seething but also plotting.

On the drive home I passed a construction site for a new office building that was nearing completion. There was a leasing sign out. On a whim, I turned into the parking lot, tracked down the owner, and asked him if he had any space left. He did and on the spot, without hesitation, I took two offices. I quit my job and on March 1, 1983 I moved in and started my own independent advisory business.

I figured my income would take a hit for awhile but I got a big surprise. People immediately started coming out of the woodwork looking for me, saying, "Roland, now that you aren't working for that brokerage firm, what should I be doing with my money?" Unbeknownst to me, the only reason they had hesitated to let me manage their money was because they weren't sure if my loyalty would be to them or the brokerage firm. Once I was on my own, they knew I would be working for them only and the better they did, the better I did.

This was positively revolutionary at the time, and my clients loved it because it removed any second-guessing about my motives. Furthermore, I could honestly and enthusiastically say, "My father owns what you own. I own what you own. My family's future is riding on the same horse as yours." Win, lose, or draw, my clients were my partners. If I failed to lead them to the promised land, I'd be going down with the ship.

Of course, my former colleagues thought I was nuts. They didn't understand money the way I had learned about it, from my family's experiences losing everything and struggling too survive. They took for granted the prosperity and peace of American life, and it only made them arrogant and greedy for more. As the saying goes, they were like bees drowning in honey.

Some of the conversation around our kitchen table growing up was not about striking it rich. It was about how lucky we were to escape being enslaved by a corrupt socialist system, or being killed. It was about hard work and clear principles. My father earned his living with his eyes and hands, which showed all the wear and tear of years coaxing beautiful shapes out of marble. Every dollar he earned was baptized by the sweat of his brow.

I came to see that all money is baptized by human struggle at one point or another. You don't have to have fled genocidal maniacs and totalitarian corruption to grasp the concept that money should be spent wisely, invested carefully, and nurtured for the long haul. My respect for money and the freedom it provides, along with my sense of fair play, are at the core of my approach to investing. There's no more magic in it than that. It's common sense that's as old as civilization.

Today, a quarter-century after I started my independent firm, it's amazing how people still make foolish choices: chasing the "new economy" of the 1990s; the sure thing of real estate; and the lure of financial "products" so complex, no one could figure out what they were worth until they were worthless. I have no doubt that tomorrow it'll be the sure thing of something else.

Throughout it all, in my seminar series, on my radio show, in consultations with clients, and now in these pages, the lessons I've been teaching on how to build and maintain wealth have not changed in 30 years. Invest in ownership positions, diversify, and let time do the rest. It's more complicated than that, which is where I earn my keep.

In the following chapter, I'll describe some of the more common mistakes we humans make with our money, give you a peek inside the investment industry to show how it exploits your emotions, and expose some of the more egregious hidden conflicts of interests. I hope it makes you as mad as it made me, because that determination is the first step toward making good choices.

Money Madness

> **Bull markets are born on pessimism, grow on skepticism, mature on optimism, and die on euphoria.**
>
> —*John Templeton*

JIMMY CARTER made a speech in early spring of 1978 that terrified me, financially speaking. New York City had been teetering on the verge of bankruptcy, interest rates were rising, unemployment was high, and gold was trading roughly around $150 an ounce, up from a low of $35. It had been six years since Nixon took the country off the gold standard, a decision I regarded as a travesty and a potential disaster.

The speech Carter gave that spooked me announced a series of government programs designed to help bail out the cities (which were in big trouble financially and in terms of quality of life), make home ownership more accessible to the poor, guarantee business loans in poor areas, and create jobs. In other words, a government spending spree.

Carter's announcement was news, but it barely created a ripple in the financial press. I was convinced that the effect of all this easier money meant the Federal Reserve would be inking up its printing presses to manufacture more currency, currency no longer backed by gold but by empty promises.

By this time I was deep into my studies of money and investing and I had no doubt that cheaper money meant only one thing: inflation. I scanned the newspapers and magazines for an article or even a letter to the editor warning about this threat and found nothing. I wondered: Am I the only person who gets this?

Finally I found someone who did, Ken Chambers of St. Louis, one of the most fluent people at the time on the subject of inflation and its relationship to the price of gold. I invited him to Omaha to speak to some of my clients and, as a result, moved my clients' portfolios to 20 percent gold, mostly in the form of gold-mining shares.

> **"You'd have thought I was selling my clients bomb shelters. Financially, I was."**

When my colleagues at the brokerage firm heard through the grapevine what I was up to, they ridiculed me, calling me a gold bug, an insulting term suggesting I was some wild-eyed, end-of-the-world lunatic. You'd have thought I was selling my clients bomb shelters. Financially, I was.

Early in 1978, Ken Chambers had written a study titled the "840 Prophecy." He predicted gold could rise as high as $840 an ounce within two years. He was right on target. Gold peaked in January 1980 at $850 an ounce. My clients and I made a fortune and the boys back at the old firm weren't laughing anymore. I had earned my stripes and made a name for myself in the community. I still have many of those clients that started with me around that time.

Gold fell after that to a low of $296 in 1982. It spiked again in January 1983 to $510, by which time, I'd sold off enough to keep it to 5 percent of the portfolio as insurance. The stock market had bottomed out in 1982 and was on a strong bull run.

Money Versus Your Brain

I had learned about a small cobalt mine in California whose shares looked historically cheap. Ordinarily I wouldn't have given it a second thought. But I happened to know that cobalt is essential in the manufacture of jet engines. I have had a lifetime love affair with airplanes, have been a longtime pilot, and had grown up in Italy near the American military airfield at Aviano.

The Reagan administration was spending a ton of money on military hardware, especially aircraft. The administration was trying to outspend the USSR and drive it into bankruptcy. Defense contractor stocks were hot.

I bought a small amount of the cobalt mine stock for clients, my father, and myself at fifty cents a share, fairly certain it could reach $5 when the rest of the world woke up and realized what was going on. Sure enough, the price blasted through $5—and kept going.

When it reached $9 a share, I told my father he should think about taking his profits. He wanted to wait a little longer. After all, it had gone up so therefore it must be going up some more! When it reached $12 a share, I went to see my father to try to talk him into selling at least some of it.

"I think it's going higher," he said, now hypnotized by the amazing price rise. "I'll sell it when it gets to $20." Not if it gets to $20, but when. He owned about 3,000 shares, so he had a huge profit, more than $30,000 which, even after taxes, was a lot of money to a marble artist.

> "He had decided it was a $20 stock and, by God, he was going to hang on until it got where he thought it should go."

When the stock reached $15 I begged him to get rid of it. "It can't go up forever, Papa." By this time I had sold all of mine and my clients' shares.

"I know," he said. "But why sell as long as it's still going up? I'm holding out for $20." I couldn't change his mind.

Predictably, the stock began to falter and then plummet. Nothing I said could convince Papa to sell. He had decided it was a $20 stock and, by God, he was going to hang on until it got where he thought it should go. After all, it had been a $15 stock and at the least it should go back to $15, right? By the time the dust settled, he sold the stock for about $1.50 a share. He'd left more than $40,000 on the table.

"In the future," my father said, "don't ask me. Just do it."

Even so-called experts can't get out of the way of their emotions. In a recent book entitled "Your Money & Your Brain," former Forbes magazine writer Jason Zweig tells the story of Harry M. Markowitz, a Nobel Prize-winning economist who is credited with co-inventing the modern theory of investing—diversification. But Markowitz, knowing what he knew, invested just like my father. He was incapable of following his own research and knowledge with his own money.

Examples abound:

- In 1979, *Business Week* magazine ran a cover story titled "The Death of Equities," suggesting that the stock market, which had been struggling for a decade to reach and exceed its old 1960s "go-go years" high of 1,000 on the Dow Jones Industrial Average, was no longer relevant. At the time, the Dow was at 800. Three years later, the longest bull market in history began.

- A well-known investment advisor tells the story of attending a conference in Italy years ago with an internationally famous economist. The two men went to dinner and when the check came, the economist was horrified at the cost, about $50. The investment advisor laughed and said, "You must be joking. A luxury meal like this would cost two or three times that in the States." To which the economist replied, "Oh, I never go out to eat." The supposed economic expert was clueless about the cost of things, living in a bubble.

- In stock market crashes like the one that occurred in October 1987, people sold because stocks were going down. They should have been buying, because the market completely recovered and went on to new highs. A large measure of the success my clients and I have enjoyed came as a result of buying when the world was selling, and selling when the world was buying. All markets decline from time to time and, as history shows, eventually recover to new highs.

  > The success my clients and I have enjoyed came mostly from buying when the world was selling, and selling when the world was buying.

- In the stock market boom of the 1990s, people bought stocks simply because stocks were going up. When a Wall Street analyst who had once been an office boy for CNN's Lou Dobbs—Henry Blodget—predicted Amazon.com shares were going to $400 from $243, the feeding frenzy drove the price to $400. Then it collapsed. Three years later, it traded around $30 and eight years later, Amazon still hasn't revisited its all-time high.

It's not just Americans who are foolish around money. Other immigrants from Italy that my family knew often kept their money in boxes and paper bags. They would show up at real estate closings with sacks full of cash. An acquaintance tells the story of having given his retired father—a New York City police officer—a thousand dollars in cash each week, so he wouldn't have to touch his pension. When his father died, he found every dollar—$175,000—in a box in a closet.

I am fully empathetic with the fear these people felt considering the experiences they'd had, which included watching banks fail during the Great Depression. But it's a shame to someone who knows they could have doubled or tripled that cash without taking much more risk than they did keeping bags full of flimsy, flammable paper around the house. Not even a safe can protect your money as well as some investments.

Many people in my generation hold attitudes about money that are based on their conception of the Great Depression. They may not have lived through it, but their parents and grandparents did and they never let the kids and grandkids forget about it. Unfortunately, what most people think they know about that time is simply wrong. Pioneer Fund, one of the oldest mutual funds in the world, started in 1928, the year before the crash. Within a few years, it had returned to its 1929 high. People forget that the 1930s saw two of the best ten years in the stock market, along with three of the worst ten.

Nevertheless, the greatest fears of people I meet are another Great Depression, and high inflation or collapse of the dollar. Gold is my hedge against high inflation and a falling dollar, and long-term government bonds are my hedge against the risk of a depression. Neither should be used as an investment, only as hedge positions. While I think the chances of financial catastrophe are small, I want to protect my money just in case.

Ratio of Stock Prices to Gold Prices Shows How Owning Gold Shares Can Protect Your Portfolio

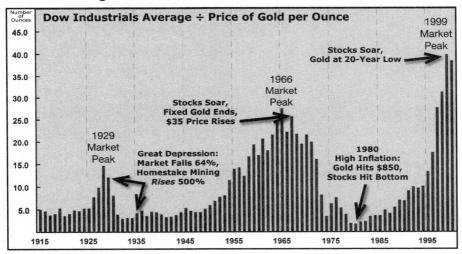

This chart shows the amount of gold in ounces (left scale) it took to theoretically "buy" the Dow Jones Industrial Average from 1915 to 2000. Clearly, the best time to buy gold shares has been when gold was cheapest relative to stocks, often just before a major market decline.

Thus, a portfolio that included some gold-mining shares would have been hedged (protected on the downside) against those bear markets. For example, the Dow Jones Industrials fell by 64% between the Crash of 1929 and December 1935, but shares of Homestake Mining, a gold producer, rose from $80 to $495, *plus* paid dividends.

After 1968, the price of gold, which had been frozen at $35 an ounce for decades, was allowed to float. Gold began to rise, peaking in 1980 at $850 during high inflation while the Dow Industrials became stalled for almost 15 years, unable to break through its 1966 high of 1,000.

A powerful bull market took off in 1982. Stocks soared and gold began to fall. By 1999, gold hit a 20-year low, less than a year before the stock market high-tech bubble began to deflate.

At the beginning of 2008, with gold trading near a new all-time high of $1,000 an ounce, the Dow/gold ratio was about 14, roughly one-third what it was in 1999. This means gold is not yet in the bargain range.

How Betty Beat Enron

I've had a client for a number of years who is famous in our offices for an investment decision she and her husband made that was so controversial she couldn't even speak of it in certain circles. Even today she prefers to keep her identity a secret. I'll call her Betty.

I met Betty through her husband, who I had known for fifteen years through a mutual interest in sports cars. Betty worked in the energy business her whole life and she had risen up the ranks from being a pipeline maintenance worker to become a manager responsible for coordinating the connection of new gas wells to the company's pipelines. She is a six-foot-tall ex-farm girl whose father had worked for the Union Pacific Railroad and grew corn.

But he died young. As the youngest child, Betty grew up in a frugal home where her mother had to keep the family together by herself. The biggest fear they faced was that a year of hard work raising a corn crop could be wiped out by a single hail storm, along with their profit.

As Betty moved up the ladder at her company, she had a traditional defined-benefit retirement plan with the funds invested in the company's stock. But then, in 1986, the company was bought out by another company whose CEO was an ambitious guy named Ken Lay. The new name on her paycheck was Enron.

Betty had no experience with investments, and Enron's stock had been going up. The gossip around her office was that the smart thing to do was nothing—leave the money invested in Enron.

In 1996, Enron introduced a new retirement plan that had the promising slogan, "Only You." Control over where the retirement funds were invested was now in the hands of the employees, and the company offered educational classes to explain to people who had little or no investment experience what their options were. Those who did nothing had their retirement fund contributions, and matching company funds, invested solely in shares of Enron.

> One night at dinner, her husband suggested that maybe it was time to take the money off the table.
> "Why would we do that?" Betty asked. "Jeff Skilling says the stock's going to $135"

Betty had no experience with investments, and Enron's stock had been going up. The gossip around her office was that the smart thing to do was nothing—leave the money invested in Enron. The company was growing rapidly, and CEO Lay and President Jeffrey Skilling had been telling workers at conferences and other events that the stock was going to eventually reach $135 a share. So she let her chips ride on Enron.

When the stock price hit $50 a share, Enron threw parties for employees in various regional offices at which every worker received a crisp new $50 bill and a pep talk: "Look what your hard work has done. With more hard work, the sky's the limit!"

The stock kept going up, and by early 1999 it reached $75 a share. Betty, the one-time pipe fitter whose father had been a engineer for the railroad, was a paper millionaire. One night at dinner, her husband suggested that maybe it was time to take the money off the table.

"Holy mackerel!" I blurted. "This is ridiculous. Not only are your fortunes completely tied to one company, the company's stock is outrageously over-priced."

"Why would we do that?" Betty asked. "Jeff Skilling says the stock's going to $135 and the company's doing really well. Nobody in my office is selling. They'd call me crazy if I did."

Because her husband knew me, he suggested we meet to get some professional advice. The day we met, I took a look at Enron's stock price and its price-to-earnings ratio, a way of valuing a stock based on the company's profitability and growth rate. I couldn't help myself. "Holy mackerel!" I blurted. "This is ridiculous. Not only are your fortunes completely tied to one company, the company's stock is outrageously over-priced."

In fact, much of the stock market was overpriced. My advice was unequivocal. Sell and put at least 80 percent of your money into a diversified portfolio. Get the hell out of Enron! I showed her how I diversified my investments and she said, "Okay. That makes sense."

Betty and her husband went home and had a family conference. She was nervous and so was he, but for opposing reasons. She was experiencing the kind of anxiety that infects investors in an upward, greedy market—money madness. The anxiety comes from the fear that by selling you lose the opportunity to make even more money if the stock goes up. It's the fear of being left behind, losing out, missing that second piece of cake—the same emotion we feel as children. Soaring prices produce soaring emotions which lead to irrational expectations and behavior, such as believing a money-losing company like

Amazon.com was worth $400 a share, or about $30 billion in total market capitalization.

To put the madness in perspective, at the same time that the mob was chasing the AOLs and Amazon.coms, oil was trading at just under $11 a barrel and Occidental Petroleum was trading at a twenty-year low, yielding a dividend of about 20 percent. A company

> **Betty was experiencing the kind of anxiety that infects investors in an upward, greedy market—money madness. The anxiety comes from the fear that by selling you lose the opportunity to make even more money if the stock goes up.**

whose dividend ratio gets that high is one whose stock has fallen because investors have lost confidence in its ability to continue paying the dividend. Occidental was struggling, but it owned a valuable commodity: oil.

In other words, an idea whose profitability had yet to be tested (Amazon) was being valued at ten times a company that had a half billion in cash in the bank and many billions worth of petroleum reserves in the ground. Money madness. Anyone who bought Occidental Petroleum in 1999 and stuck with it would have earned 20 percent a year on their principal, plus a six-fold increase in their original investment. A dollar invested in Occidental in 1998-1999 would have grown to about $10 today.

My father had succumbed to a similar emotion. His fear was that if he sold as the stock fell, it would go back up and he would have lost the opportunity to recoup the "losses" he had experienced, even though he was way ahead of where he started. He never "lost" a cent on his investment. In fact, he made a nice profit, on a percentage basis. But he became wedded to the idea that the stock was worth some imaginary value and, maybe by force of will, he thought he could get it to go back up.

Betty and her husband came to an agreement. They would sell the Enron and let me diversify the proceeds. When they came in Betty told me, "We shook hands on it. If the price collapses, he won't say 'I told you so.' If the price goes way up, I won't blame him for letting the big one get away."

I assured them both that either way, they were making a smart move. But when Betty went back to the office and told her colleagues what she'd done, and handed out some of my literature, she got an odd reaction. They looked at her as if she'd lost her mind.

"Why the heck would you do something like that?" they asked, voices tinged with outrage—who the hell did she think she was? "The stock is going to $135. Jeff Skilling's told us that a hundred times. You're gonna be mighty sorry you did that." Betty was shocked at their comments, and even a little embarrassed. But her retirement fund was no longer tied to the fortunes of one company.

The only person in the office who followed Betty's advice was a secretary nearing retirement. Cashing out made perfect sense for a person at her stage of life. But the others hung on. The stock continued to rise for another year or so, peaking at $90 a share. Betty endured the told-you-so taunts of her co-workers, until the price started to backslide.

Some of Betty's colleagues sold a little of their stock, to pay off mortgages, fund college educations, and buy new cars and other toys. But as the stock continued to fall, Enron's executives continued to beat the drums of optimism and instead of getting the hint, the employees bought more stock. Co-workers who retired took their Enron stock with them and held on to it.

Nobody wanted to be left behind when the stock got to $135.

By 2001, the full disaster of Enron was beginning to reveal itself and the mood in Betty's office had deteriorated from euphoric to depressed to paralyzed. Coworkers who had made the mistake of holding on and riding the stock all the way down began to treat her like she had leprosy. She kept her mouth shut around new people who came to work, preferring they think she was working because she, too, had lost her retirement and needed the income.

Those who had been driven mad by their greed and anxiety resented the fact that, at the age of sixty, Betty had the peace of mind of knowing she could quit anytime and be set for life.

But she kept working only because she wanted to stay busy. Those who had been driven mad by their greed and anxiety resented the fact that, at the age of sixty, Betty had the peace of mind of knowing she could quit anytime and be set for life. They were envious, and she was a daily reminder of what had been in their grasp but they lost by ignoring her advice. They shunned her.

As we all know now, Enron went broke amid a huge accounting scandal and its remaining assets were picked up at fire sales by other companies. Now Betty's company is owned by Warren Buffett's holding company, Berkshire Hathaway, and her reinvested Enron money that was diversified has nearly doubled. Betty occasionally runs into a former co-worker manning a register at the check-out counter at the supermarket or in some similar job, and the conversation, whenever there is one, is awkward at best.

There is no perfect time to sell a winning investment, and it's the rare case that anyone manages to pick a top. But if you ever get that anxious feeling that you might be missing out on a bigger profit than the one you have, that might be a good time to check your emotions.

I have several ceramic pigs on my desk to remind me of an old Wall Street adage: bulls make money, bears make money, but pigs get slaughtered.

You and Money

> ❝ **A goal without a plan is just a wish.** ❞
>
> —*Antoine de Saint-Exupery, French writer (1900–1944)*

MOST PEOPLE I meet are confused about money in some way. I can't blame them. Everywhere you turn, someone, some media outlet, or some company is shouting at you about the "best" investments and the "right" way to invest. And you'd better hurry! You might miss out on a good thing.

Everywhere you turn, there is another investment company or bank promising "independent" "objective" advice that will lead to such utter peace of mind that all its happy clients can spend the rest of their care-free lives looking tanned and healthy as they travel around the world on their yachts or just lounge by the beach in front of their oceanside mansions.

Articles in magazines and on websites shout about the " Must-own mutual funds for retirement;" the "10 high-quality, low-risk stocks to ride out the current turbulence;" the "Under valued market sectors you need to know about;" how to live debt-free; how to retire with a million dollars—on and on it goes.

There are two problems with all of this racket. The first

You can find bad advice just about anywhere, from the personal finance pages of The Wall Street Journal to television celebrities like Suze Orman and Jim Cramer.

is that there is no one-size-fits-all solution, so all this advice only serves to make people anxious that they're missing out on something, or that they've made a terrible mistake. Add to the confusion the fear that's fanned by the constant drum-beat in the media about Social Security going broke, Boomers unprepared for retirement, housing market collapses, and all the other calamities-du-jour magnified to keep you glued to your tv set. These emotions are what drive people to make bad decisions.

The second problem is that much of the hype and advice is too general, conflicting, or just plain wrong. You can find bad advice just about anywhere, from the Personal Finance pages of *The Wall Street Journal* to television celebrities like Suze Orman and Jim Cramer.

Most of the advice dished out is empty calories and often presented as the gospel truth. But there is no such thing as gospel truth because everyone's situation is unique and no one investment is right unless it is considered within an investment plan.

Bad Ideas From The "Experts"

Sometimes these pundits give out patently bad advice that, if you followed it, could rob you of future wealth. Some have advocated, for example, that people invest retirement funds in a Roth IRA rather than a traditional IRA. This is a classic example of conventional wisdom that is the exact opposite of what just about everyone should do.

The money you put in a Roth IRA is after you've paid your taxes, which means that up to 35 percent (the current maximum federal tax rate) of your money is gone right off the top, plus state taxes. That thirty-five cents will never earn you a single cent. It now belongs to your government to squander as it sees fit. This is simple mathematics. Instead of investing a dollar, you've only invested sixty-five cents.

The supposed advantage of a Roth is that when you retire, you can withdraw the money tax-free—pay now, save later. This might make sense if you're young and paying taxes at the lowest rate, and "plan" to retire rich when your tax rate will be high. Unless you have magic powers to predict the future, this could be a risky bet.

In any case, when most people retire their expenses will have dropped (kids are grown, downsizing the house, widowed, and so on) and they won't need as much money to live, and they'll probably be in a lower tax bracket. So what you save tomorrow is unlikely to ever match what you gave up today.

With a traditional IRA, every dollar you put in is untaxed. That means that every dollar goes to work for you from day one, day in and day out, year in and year out, until you need it. Every dollar that that dollar earns will be compounding for you. On the basis of compound interest alone, a traditional IRA makes sense more often than not.

The advice from Roth advocates gets worse when you consider that, because of the inevitable erosion of inflation, today's dollar is always going to have more buying power than any dollar you receive in the future. For example, a dollar today can be expected in ten years to have only 66 cents of buying power, assuming inflation remains around its historical average.

Another thing that the experts of the world tell their audiences is that they should strive to pay off their home mortgages. This is, for most people and most of the time, a wasteful use of money.

Then there is the unpredictability of government tax laws. There are proposals for a flat tax, or a national sales tax. We might not even have an income tax someday.

Since no one can predict the future, it's just common sense to take advantage of the deductible benefit you are given today.

You are better off investing all of a stronger dollar today using a traditional IRA, and paying taxes years later with a dollar that will have been devalued by inflation.

Another thing that the financial pundits of the world tell their audiences is that they should strive to pay off their home mortgages. This is, for most people and most of the time, a wasteful use of money. It's simple math.

When you pay back the principal you borrowed to buy your home you are locking your wealth up in your house, which will increase in value—on average—about the same as inflation. Although we did experience a real estate bubble after the stock market bubble, it burst. Once the dust clears, real estate can be expected to return to more typical growth rates. This means you'll not grow any wealthier, just not any poorer.

The concept is as simple as the one I explained years ago to my stock broker boss, Ron. When you can borrow from the bank at four to five percent (a six-percent mortgage minus the interest deduction tax break), and put that money to work in a diversified portfolio of equity mutual funds that historically have averaged 10 to 12 percent, you don't need any degrees or special powers to figure out the better choice.

My Favorite Misconceptions

In my years as an investment advisor, I've heard just about every misconception, misunderstanding, and bad idea anyone ever had about you and your money. Here are a few of my favorites:

- I'm going to put money in the stock market but I want to wait for it to go up some more. (This is the "I'll do it if everybody else does" approach—follow the mob.) Would you buy a house this way?

- I know the stock I own is down to $40 a share but it's been as high as $90, so it's got to be worth at least that much. I'm gonna hold on 'til it goes back up.

- The stock market returns 10 percent a year.

- Wall Street is just a gambling pit.

- Paying cash is the secret to wealth.

- CDs, bonds, and fixed annuities are the safest investments because your principal is guaranteed.

- Subtract your age from 100 to get the percentage you should have in stocks.

- Inflation equals rising prices.

- Always pay off your mortgage before anything else.

- Annuities provide "Stock market returns with no risk." (Verbatim from an annuity ad.)

- You need a high paying job to become financially independent.
- All debt is bad.
- I don't have enough money to invest.
- Life insurance is a good investment.

By the time you get to the end of this book, you'll understand that every one of these comments or beliefs is in one way or another flawed and can rob you of your future financial peace of mind.

Planning to Grow Wealth

People who have serious money to protect and grow are starting to get wise to Wall Street and its self-serving system of managing your money. Meanwhile, Wall Street has shown its gratitude to the investing public by throwing the little guys overboard because their accounts aren't big enough to make money on.

Goliaths like Merrill Lynch have raised the amount you need to have in your account in order to be able to talk to a real stock broker. Instead, those unlucky customers are directed to a web site or a call center in some faraway place like Bangalore. You have to be a whale to get attention these days from the traditional investment industry.

The good news is that there is a growing army of independent advisors who have followed the path I took years ago, leaving the ranks of the Great Powers of Wall Street so they can offer truly objective advice. But advice is useful only in the context of a plan and it always surprises me how many people don't have a plan. They have goals—vacations, second homes, bequests, philanthropy, and so on—but they haven't sat down and figured out if and how those goals are reachable.

Choose An Advisor Like a Doctor

Choosing an investment advisor should be approached as a major decision, not unlike choosing a doctor. Like medical advice, financial advice is not just about the issue at hand, but about counseling and guidance. Barbara Kahn, a professor of marketing at the Wharton School of Business, conducted research in 2006 into how consumers make important health care decisions. She found that patients had no trouble identifying the most important factors—quality of life, survival rates, and cost—but they struggled to express them in a single value.

> Choosing an investment advisor should be approached as a major decision, not unlike choosing a doctor. Like medical advice, financial advice is not just about the issue at hand, but about counseling and guidance.

The choices that must be made around financial advice are similar to health care in that they are often unpleasant and anxiety-producing, and difficult to express in a single value. When it comes to money, people often feel almost as vulnerable as they do about health. They want someone who can help them make good choices. They want someone who will not just listen, but collaborate.

If you ask most investment advisors today, "How can you help me?" they will usually launch into a discussion about annuities, mutual funds, or some investment strategy. The correct answer is that financial advisors and wealth managers should help people preserve and grow their buying power, match their financial needs with their life choices, and show them how to manage their emotions so they can make smart choices.

This is not just good for investors, it also turns out to be good for investment advisors. CEG Research, a consulting firm catering to the financial advisor industry, recently completed a study for Dow Jones & Co. of more than 2,000 top wealth managers and found that those who spent time developing close client relationships earn three times as much as traditional advisors. "Only a small group of advisors (about 6 percent) truly practice the relationship-oriented approach that defines wealth management."

I've been practicing this "religion" for all the years I've been in the wealth management business and I have heard my share of sad cases of people who didn't get the care and attention they deserved. I find most people are so confused about money and investments that they often don't know whether or not their investments are diversified, or even what their rate of return has been.

> **Intelligence has nothing to do with whether a person is smart or dumb about money.**

Intelligence has nothing to do with whether a person is smart or dumb about money. An acquaintance in the wealth management field tells the story of two thirty-something dot-com entrepreneurs—former college buddies—who built a company in which their stakes were worth $350 million each. Fame and fortune had

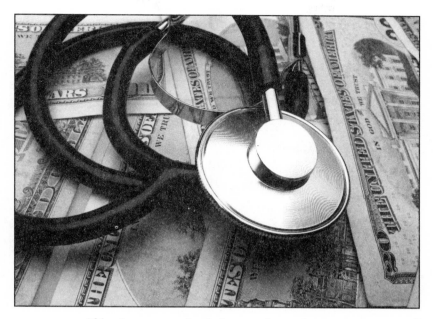

come so swiftly they never had time to learn how to manage all that wealth. They had achieved the American dream and discovered it comes with ropes attached.

As their company became more successful, they gave in to just about every pitch by brokers who came along peddling the latest hot ideas or investment products. Like squirrels burying nuts all around the forest floor, they had a notion that diversification meant doling out a few million here and a few million there to each in a parade of brokers from brand-name firms. Thrown in for good measure were some old college chums who had gone into the investment business and showed up on their doorstep eager to "help" a fellow alum.

The rationale for this approach had been to create a horse race—give some money to competing firms to see who produced the best results. The unintended outcome was that they were essentially betting against themselves, like simultaneously playing black and red on the roulette wheel. The "00" guarantees

It dawned on these two fellows that, like squirrels, they had no clue where their money was, how much they were worth, nor whether any particular investment was ahead or behind.

that, in the end, the house (the brokerage industry) wins.

With no coordination in their investments, they exposed themselves to the risk that their competing brokers were all chasing the same fad, or making opposing trades. These successful entrepreneurs were too busy doing what they did best to stop, study, and supervise their investments. Some of their brokers had been taking full advantage by investing the money in mutual funds and other vehicles that yielded the brokers the highest commissions or offered them some other incentive, like a free trip to a mutual fund "educational" conference on Maui.

It slowly dawned on these two fellows that, just like squirrels, they had no clue where all their money was, how much they were worth, nor whether any particular investment was ahead or behind. Their mailboxes overflowed each month with an avalanche of account statements and confirmation notices. Each partner had a US Postal Service plastic bin into which they pitched it all without looking. Then the bins were carted off once a month to the accountants whose job was to record all the data, but without analyzing it. Nobody was paying attention.

When they finally capitulated and handed over those bins to an objective investment advisor, they discovered that one of the brokers had sold stock in one company only to turn around and buy shares in its parent corporation. This had triggered capital gains taxes on the sale, and they'd essentially bought back what they'd sold, paying commissions on both transactions. The account statements told an expensive and sorry tale of clumsy and questionable decisions.

All of this chaos—fed by the collapse of the 1990s technology bubble—had shrunk their net worth to about $25 million each. They might have been the smartest guys in the room in their field, but that intelligence had proved useless when it came to money. They had lost more than 90 percent of the wealth they had created.

Even clients I have gotten to know and had the chance to educate—people with whom I've spent a great deal of time planning—still succumb to their worst impulses. It's not uncommon for longtime clients to one day walk in to the office and announce that they bought something on their own a few weeks back that they heard about from family or friends, and now they want us to explain to them what it is! Yet not a one of them would ever consider buying a house before it had been thoroughly inspected.

Wise Counsel

The first job of an investment advisor is to maximize returns after all taxes, fees, and inflation. Too often, people get advice from their accountants that works against this goal. Accountants play an important role on your financial team but many are trained to pay attention to taxes and almost nothing more. It often happens that an

> **The first job of an investment advisor is to maximize returns after taxes, fees, and inflation. People often get advice from accountants that works against this goal.**

accountant will discourage a client from selling an investment solely because of capital gains taxes, only to see that investment go down the tubes. Sometimes it's better to take your profits and pay the piper.

I often meet people who have been sold an annuity without having a single clue how it works. (I have strong opinions about annuities, which I detail in Chapter 9.) The annuity salesperson may have told them how it works but the customers weren't paying attention because it was boring or confusing. Chances are good the salesperson didn't understand it either, and was just parroting the marketing line handed him by the insurance company. The prospectuses for some annuities can be hundreds of pages long. How could anyone understand what the product is?

> **In my decades in business, I have seen a lot of odd and counter-intuitive behavior around money.**

In my experience, people want direction, not choices they can't evaluate.

Money Psychology

In my decades in business, I have seen a lot of odd and counter-intuitive behavior around money. I have had many clients who spent years saving and living below their means and retired so wealthy that their investment portfolio could pay them more than they ever earned in their careers. But they were stuck in the saver mentality and were afraid to start spending. As politely as I can, I challenge them: what was the point of sacrificing all those years if you can't let yourself enjoy the payoff?

At the other end of the spectrum are those who have put hardly anything away and one day wind up with a big inheritance. They think they're all set for retirement and I have to break the news to them that it isn't quite that easy. I show them how little they will be able to spend each year to keep from running out of money. But they still think and spend as if they won the lottery.

To talk them "off the ledge" I walk them through the math, showing that an annual withdrawal of 5 percent of their portfolio's value is a safe place to start. I explain that they need to keep 95 percent working for them so their portfolio can keep up with and hopefully beat inflation.

There are so many ways wealth is frittered away. We investment advisors repeatedly encounter the phenomenon of "shirtsleeves to shirtsleeves in three generations." It has been estimated that as much as 70 percent of wealth is dissipated within three generations of its creation.

It has been estimated that as much as 70 percent of wealth is dissipated within three generations of its creation.

One of the most frequently cited examples is the Vanderbilt family. Cornelius Vanderbilt, the man who created a transportation empire from scratch, died in 1877 with an estate three times larger than Bill Gates's estimated wealth, adjusted for inflation. When 120 Vanderbilt heirs got together for a reunion almost a century later, there wasn't a single millionaire among them.

In a period when a growing number of people are experiencing sudden wealth—from entrepreneurs to professional athletes—stories of squandered good fortune are becoming more common. There are, by some estimates, more than nine million households in the US with a net worth—not including the value of their primary residence—of $1 million or more. Americans are adept at creating value and wealth, but often have a hard time holding on to it.

A Big Salary Is Not Wealth

Too many people think wealth comes from a large income. It's not how much you earn, it's what you do with what you earn. I've had many clients who've earned very low salaries their entire careers but wound up millionaires because of their lifelong saving and investing habits. On the other hand, there are those who have advanced degrees and high-paying jobs but have nothing to show but fancy houses and expensive toys.

Most people have no clue how much their retirement is going to cost them. They think the correct goal is to retire being able to maintain their current standard of living. To do that, one needs roughly twenty times that annual amount in a nest egg to provide adequate income with inflation protection, assuming your portfolio is your only source of income. This is not a rule, but a general guide.

> I've had 55 year olds come in with $50,000 and declare that they'd like to retire in 10 years. It'd be funny if it wasn't so sad.

I've had 55 year olds come in with $50,000 and declare that they'd like to retire in 10 years. It'd be funny if it wasn't so sad. I try to explain reality without putting too great a scare into them. This doesn't make them feel good, but that's the big difference between someone whose interests are aligned with yours and a salesperson for a brokerage firm or an insurance company. The salesperson tells you what's going to make you feel good so you'll buy what they're peddling and they can earn their commission. Your future is not part of that equation.

The High Cost of Panic

One of the constant conversations I have with clients has to do with quieting their fears during dramatic shifts in the markets, and the media hysteria they generate. When people call in a panic after a market break or some other seeming calamity, I ask them, "Did you go to work today and continue producing?"

Of course, they say.

"So did the rest of America," I say, "and eventually we will get through this patch like we always do. Every year there is something to panic about. But over the long haul, with knowledge and discipline, you'll come out ahead."

Measure to Manage

Whether you manage your own investments or you've found an investment advisor you trust, it's an important exercise to keep track of where you are so you know what your options are in the future. In the pages that follow you'll find the Confidential Financial Planning Guide I developed for clients many years ago. I encourage you to photocopy it and fill it in.

The purpose is to calculate your net worth, an exercise you should repeat once every year, around tax time when most of us have our records all together anyway. This is a simple way for you to gauge where you are on the path to financial independence, and to keep track of whether goals and your resources are matching up. If you can't measure it, you can't manage it.

Once you know where you are, the next step is to re-educate yourself about how money works. Once you do, you've got the secret weapon to cut through all the noise and make the best choices every time. Pencils ready?

Confidential Financial Planning Guide

Use the information you develop for this form to assess your life goals as it relates to your financial life, where you are in the cycle of life, where you want to go from here, and then you can begin the discussion of how you get there.

You will find a printer-friendly version of the following form online at: www.Manarin.com/financial_planning.

Date:_____

(1)   Family Information

Name_____Age_____
Spouse's name_____Age_____
Address _____
City_____State____Zip_____
Phone (Home)_____
        (Cell)_____
        (Work)_____
Your occupation_____
Employer_____
Your SS#_____
Your date of birth_____
Spouse's occupation_____
Employer_____
Spouse's SS#_____
Spouse's date of birth_____

Children's names	Age	Dependent
_____	_____	Y N
_____	_____	Y N
_____	_____	Y N
_____	_____	Y N

Your Advisory Team:
Banker_____
      Phone_____
CPA/Accountant_____
      Phone_____
Attorney_____
      Phone_____
Insurance Agent_____
      Phone_____

Do you have a will?_____
Date of your will_____
Do you have a trust?_____
Date of your trust_____

Have you used tax shelters?   Y   N
To what extent?_____
_____
_____

Do you expect any inheritances?
Husband: Y   N   Estimated $_____
Wife: Y   N   Estimated $_____

(2)   Personal Financial Objectives
(Rank by Importance)
☐ Income now
☐ Long-term growth
☐ Income at retirement
☐ Build an education fund
☐ Reduce tax burden
☐ Other

If retirement is your goal:

How many years before retirement?_____
Desired monthly income at retirement?_____
Sources of monthly retirement income:
        Social security: $_____
        Company pension: $_____
        Other (Keogh, Annuities, etc): $_____
Additional income needed to meet retirement
        goal: $_____

If education of children is your goal:

Name of child	Yrs. before college	Educational goal
_____	_____	$_____
_____	_____	$_____
_____	_____	$_____
_____	_____	$_____

(3)   Current Income & Expenses

Monthly income – husband	$_____
Monthly income – wife	$_____
Other income (rent, etc)	$_____
Monthly expenses	$_____
Top tax bracket	_____%
Taxes paid last year	$_____
Amount I/we could save per month	$_____

(4)   Liabilities

Creditor	Amount	$/mo.	Interest rate
_____	$_____	$_____	_____%
_____	$_____	$_____	_____%
_____	$_____	$_____	_____%
_____	$_____	$_____	_____%
_____	$_____	$_____	_____%
Total Liabilities	$_____	$_____	

Asset Inventory

(5a) Fixed Dollars   *Owner   **(5b) Real Estate**

Checking accounts	$_____ ___	Estimated value of home	$_____
Savings accounts	$_____ ___	Remaining mortgage	$_____
Money market accts.	$_____ ___	Interest rate _____ %	
Money owed you	$_____ ___	Yrs. remaining _____ yrs.	
CD's – mature____	$_____ ___	Monthly payment $_____	
CD's – mature____	$_____ ___	Equity in home	$_____
Municipal bonds	$_____ ___	(market value-mortgage)	
Corporate bonds	$_____ ___	Other real estate	$_____
Government bonds	$_____ ___		
**Total Fixed Dollars $_____		****Total Real Estate**	$_____

(5c) Variable Dollars (Stocks, Mutual Funds, & Retirement Plans)

Company	*Owner	Date Bought	# Shares	Cost	Market Value

**Total Value of Variable Dollars $_____

(5d) Present Life Insurance & Annuities

Company	Type	Face Amount	Cash Value	Annual Premium	*Owner	Beneficiary
**Total		$_____	$_____	$_____		

(6) Other Insurance (Long-Term Care, Disability, Health)

Company	Type	Benefit	Deductible	Premium	*Owner

(7) Total $_____ - Total $_____ = Net Worth $_____

      Assets   Liabilities

*Owner: Indicate Husband (H), Wife (W), Joint Tenancy (JT), Community Property (CP), Custodial (CUST).

PART II:

The Secret Life of Money

4

Rules of the Money Game

> ❝ **The safest long-term investment for the preservation of buying power clearly has been a diversified portfolio of equities.** ❞
>
> —*Prof. Jeremy Siegel, author of "Stocks for the Long Run"*

ONE OF THE FAMILY stories I inherited from my father often comes in handy when I'm trying to help people reorient the way they think about and handle money. It's an old-country tale with a message as fresh as this morning's dew.

My father grew up near the Jizera Mountains, running along the border between Poland and modern-day Czech Republic. The mountains were also a vacation destination for the well-to-do, and he had occasion to mingle with a group of young people from wealthy families who, in the post-World War I years, would go skiing at an exclusive local resort.

That all ended in 1923 when Germany refused to continue paying France for the damage caused by the Weimar Republic starting World War I. France retaliated by invading Germany's industrial heartland—the coal-rich Ruhr Valley—to "collateralize" the debt. The Ruhr Crisis, as it came to be known, decimated the economies of Germany and its eastern neighbors.

During the 1923-1924 hyperinflation crisis in Germany, paper currency was worth so little that it was cheaper to burn it as fuel than to use it to buy firewood. (Photo courtesy of Wikipedia Commons. © AdsD der Friedrich-Ebert-Stiftung)

Inflation soared and paper money lost most of its buying power. Kids in the skiing group found themselves suddenly poor, and were no longer seen racing down the slopes or sipping aperitifs in the cafes.

Like many of the others, one of these was a young woman who had been living on a fortune inherited from her industrialist father, who died when she was quite young. The estate had been kept in "safe" German investments, based in marks, that had imploded and become worthless. Her bank account no longer had any buying power and she faced the very future from which her father had tried to protect her.

With time on her hands, scrounging for possessions

she might be able to sell, she was cleaning out a drawer in her father's old desk one day when she found a packet of documents, tied up in a small portfolio with a ribbon. Inside were beautifully engraved stock certificates. Having no experience with investments, she thought about tossing them out since they were probably as worthless as everything else. But she decided to have them looked at anyway.

I found it interesting that people had put their faith in the currency issued by their government, and then were betrayed.

It turned out that she owned large positions in several companies that not only survived the Ruhr Crisis, but prospered. As suddenly as she had become poor, she was once again wealthy.

As bad as the Great Depression was, it's hard to imagine an economic catastrophe causing more misery than the Ruhr Crisis—it set in motion the events leading to World War II and the Holocaust. What I found interesting was that people who had put their faith in the currency issued by their government had been betrayed. It was as if they had lent money to the government and instead of earning interest, they had to pay it in the form of constantly rising prices and constantly devaluing currency.

But those dusty old stock certificates shoved in a drawer were evidence of ownership that turned out to be worth more than a bank vault full of deflated paper money. Owning gold at that time was an even safer investment. The message I got from this story was clear: the safest place for money is the one that makes you an owner, not a lender.

The Three States of Money

Venita VanCaspel, a financial writer I admire, wrote a number of books in which she talked about money in terms of the three ways you can use it. In her 1978 book, "The New Money Dynamics," she discussed money in the context of its three principal uses: you can spend, lend, or own.

Three decades of studying behavior around money has convinced me that success in building and preserving wealth requires an understanding of these three states of money, so we can choose the right one in any situation. Most of us are some of each, but very few people comprehend how those options interact to determine our financial future and our ability to achieve financial independence.

A spender is just what it sounds like: someone who exhausts all their income without regard for the future. A spender might buy an antique car and trick himself into thinking it's an investment. But that person is still a spender, unless he or she is in the antique car business and knows they are getting a good deal on a car that can be readily sold at a profit.

Same thing applies to jewelry or fine art or any similar luxury goods. A spender may spoil him or herself with vacations, cars, boats, and so on. No one needs a lesson in economics to understand that spending depletes wealth, whether it's a daily latte or a forty-foot cabin cruiser.

> **A spender may buy an antique car and trick himself into thinking it's an investment. But that person is still a spender.**

Most people who think of themselves as a saver don't realize that they are actually a lender when they deposit their money in an institution such as a government, insurance company, or bank that pays you interest. When you buy a bank CD, corporate bond, or fixed annuity, you are lending money to a business that will use your money to make money for its shareholders.

If you have a money market account or bank savings account, you are also effectively a lender. That's because a bank where people park their cash turns around and can lend out many more dollars for each dollar they borrowed from you.

So your dollar that's sitting in a bank CD earning a couple percent (before the cost of taxes and the erosion of inflation) allows the bank to generate interest income for itself at whatever the competitive rate is for mortgage, car, construction, business, and other loans—many times over.

They get to do this because the Federal Reserve allows it, so long as the bank meets the requirement of only lending money to people and businesses who are likely to pay it back.

Where does the extra money the bank lends out come from? They borrow it from the Federal Reserve at favorable rates, and if the Federal Reserve doesn't have enough money to meet the demand, they just print some more.

As G. Edward Griffin, a political commentator and author of the best-selling *"The Creature from Jekyll Island,"* notes, "It doesn't take a genius to figure out that charging interest on money created from nothing is a very lucrative business model."

"It doesn't take a genius to figure out that charging interest on money created from nothing is a very lucrative business model."

That's why in recent years a new bank branch seems to have opened on every corner. All a banker has to do is open up shop, announce they have money to lend, and watch the profits roll in.

So why put money in banks and other lending vehicles? It's the safest place if you'll need the money soon. If you're shopping for a house, you'd want to put the cash you need for the down-payment and closing costs someplace where you have a guarantee it'll be there when you need it. You wouldn't put next September's college tuition into an aggressive equity mutual fund that could lose value if the stock market hiccups in the next year. Money should generally be lent if you know you'll need it within the next year or two. Beyond two years, lending is a poor choice.

The Ownership Imperative

Unfortunately, the financial industry has done a good job of convincing people to lend by arguing that having a large chunk of your money in "safe" investments is a form of diversification. I disagree, and I've made my clients and myself a great deal of money by practicing what I preach—the wealth building power of being an owner instead of a lender.

Ownership means controlling tangible assets (as opposed to dollar-based assets). Your broker or advisor may say you "own" bonds, but you don't actually own anything except the promise of the borrower, whether it's the government or a corporation, to pay you interest and eventually the principal. But they won't replace the lost buying power that inflation stole from you while they were using your money.

> Your broker or advisor may say you "own" bonds, but you don't actually own anything except the promise of the borrower

When you purchase real estate, precious metals, natural resources, and shares of stock, you are an owner. Unlike a bond or bank CD, stock shares are not a claim on paper money but a claim on the assets and future cash flow of a company. Whether you own one share or a hundred shares of a public company, you can go over to the headquarters or the factory, watch your money at work, and know that you own a piece of everything you see.

If you've chosen a diversified portfolio of good companies and you are patient, your money will go to work making more money for you instead of for your bank or insurance company.

Ownership is the key to building long-term wealth and has been since the dawn of civilization.

The 60/40 Myth

Money is confusing to most people and Wall Street has done a good job of exploiting that confusion by offering simple-sounding decisions. One of the most common is the notion that there is such a thing as the "perfect" mix of stocks and bonds that offers the "safety" of bonds with the chance to grow wealth (as opposed to just earning interest) by owning stocks.

Even some of the smartest people in the world let themselves be lulled into adopting this overly-simplified approach. You hear it all the time, read it all the time: a good retirement portfolio is about 60 percent invested in stocks and 40 percent invested in bonds.

A leading investment manager we know of who handles billions of dollars for universities and family foundations—serious money—complains that the majority of the trustees respon-

Creating and preserving wealth isn't a thermostat that you can just turn up or down depending on the weather.

sible for all this wealth seem to have drunk the same Kool-Aid as the man in the street. "They think 60/40, stocks to bonds, is the sweet spot, and if they are feeling a little conservative, they just turn the dial back to 55/45, and if they're feeling frisky, they dial it up a notch to 65/35. Then they go golfing, thinking they've done their solemn fiduciary duty."

A variation for the individual investor sounds like a joke at first: the percentage of your investment wealth you should have in stocks is arrived at by subtracting your age from 100. At age 60, the theory goes, you should have only 40 percent of your wealth in the stock market because you might need the rest in a hurry if you get sick, and you want to be able to take a spectacular retirement vacation without worrying about having money to live on when you return.

If you don't know better, the explanation is nice and neat and sort of makes sense. As you get closer to retirement (or post-primary-career years), you should reduce the risk of stock market ups and downs and increase the safety and liquidity (quick access to your cash). There is an element of truth in the idea, but creating and preserving wealth isn't a thermostat that you can just turn up or down depending on the weather.

How the Federal Reserve Caused the Depression

My interest in gold stems in part from our family experience fleeing confiscation and totalitarianism. Owning gold gave us the ability to keep our bellies full in Italy while we waited for Papa to raise the money so we could all follow him to America. Like many willing immigrants, I grew up proud to be an American and wanting to know everything I could about its history.

I studied all the major political/historical writings and documents of the country, learning about the Continental Dollar and how it became worthless. I read Thomas Jefferson's passionate argument for making gold our currency.

By 1965, when I was in college, I was way ahead of my classmates in basic economic history when a professor began a discussion one day in class about the Federal Reserve System. I worked my way through school and rarely got a proper night's sleep, so I always sat in the front row where it was harder to nod off.

I perked up as the professor went on describing how the Federal Reserve System was created in 1913 to act as the lender of last resort in case of a financial crisis. Until that time, there had been periodic panics, as they called big sell-offs in those days, that threatened to bring down the whole economy until private investors stepped in to save the day.

The reason I perked up was because I knew from my studies that, in the minds of many experts with whom I agreed, the Federal Reserve is an unconstitutional, private cartel that helped create the bubble of the 1920s, and then helped start and make the Great Depression worse than it would have been if they'd minded their own business.

> The Federal Reserve is an unconstitutional, private cartel that helped create the bubble of the 1920s, and then helped make the Great Depression worse.

The Fed was supposed to improve the movement of money in the nation, and it was granted a tool by the federal government to create money out of thin air. In the 1920s, the Fed printed too much money and that helped create the bubble. To combat the wave of speculation, the money supply growth was slowed and that led to the 1929 Crash. Every time the Fed prints more paper money and puts it into the economy through its member banks, all dollars lose some of their buying power and that's what causes inflation.

I raised my hand that day in class and asked my professor, "Isn't the Federal Reserve unconstitutional?"

He gave me a funny look and said, "Yeah, it is. How did you know?"

"Well, in Article I, Section 8 of the Constitution, it says only Congress has the right to coin money and regulate its value. So the Fed is unconstitutionally printing and distributing paper money."

"You are absolutely right," he said in a matter-of-fact tone, and then resumed his lecture.

That was the last he spoke of it, but in the years since, more people have begun to understand and pay closer attention to the actions of the Federal Reserve because it is has caused so much erosion in the value of our money. I often tell younger generations that someday everyone will drive $100,000 cars but they won't be called Porsches or Mercedes. They will be called Ford and Chevy.

> **Someday everyone will drive a $100,000 car, but they won't be called Porsches or Mercedes. They will be called Fords and Chevys.**

Why does this all matter to you today? Because if you understand that your government is allowing your paper money—called "fiat" money because it has no real value—to constantly lose buying power year after year, you'll understand why you shouldn't lend too many of those dollars in the form of a bank CD or similar vehicle where there's no opportunity for growing wealth.

Roosevelt's Great Betrayal

Once upon a time, it made sense as people aged to keep the bulk of their wealth in cash and bonds. People died younger, there were fewer choices in terms of mutual funds and other growth-oriented investments, stock market trading was harder to do and much more costly, and it was easier to get cheated. Paper currency was backed by gold and even though the price of gold didn't change, it was a tangible asset you could demand at the government's treasury window.

Things began to change during the Great Depression when President Roosevelt ordered the confiscation of all caches of gold coins and bullion. People were ordered under severe penalty to surrender their gold to the government in exchange for paper currency at the rate of $20.67 an ounce. Private ownership of gold, except for industrial use and in art, was limited to a few ounces per person. It became, in effect, illegal to own gold.

Once all the gold that people were willing to admit owning had been bought up (the smart ones hid theirs at home), the US Treasury raised the price of gold to $35 an ounce. That meant the paper dollars people got in exchange for the real thing—gold—were suddenly worth only 60 cents. The government had confiscated wealth, devalued the buying power of the dollar, betrayed the public, and prolonged the Depression.

Meanwhile, the federal government reaped an overnight

bonanza: the gold it paid $20.67 an ounce to buy could now, with the mere stroke of a pen, purchase $35 worth of goods on the international market, a 69 percent windfall profit. Revolutions have been started for less.

Almost forty years later, in 1971, President Nixon delivered the coup de grace by declaring the federal government would no longer convert dollars to gold at the fixed price of $35 an ounce. America went off the gold standard and a dollar officially became just a fancy piece of paper with a vague promise on it that has been slowly broken over the years by inflation.

> **America went off the gold standard and a dollar officially became just a fancy piece of paper with a vague promise on it that has been slowly broken over the years by government-sponsored inflation.**

I anticipated the huge rise in the price of precious metals because I was sure the Federal Reserve would have to crank up its printing presses to meet President Carter's request for money to fund all his social programs.

How Inflation Changes Everything

Thus the Federal Reserve, an unconstitutional entity that operates with government blessing and control, deliberately creates inflation, destroying the value of money. If you are "saving" money by lending it to banks and insurance companies, you are in effect buying a share of America that is guaranteed to lose value and rob you of buying power. Not much of an investment, is it?

How Inflation Steals Buying Power

This graph shows the steady erosion of buying power of a dollar since 1934, when the Federal government outlawed virtually all private ownership of gold. The spike that followed the Crash of 1929 shows a period of deflation, when prices were declining due to the Great Depression. In all, from 1914 until 2005, the buying power of a dollar has fallen by 96% to four cents.

How come Congress doesn't get rid of the Federal Reserve? Because by printing more currency, the Fed gives politicians the money to pay for goods and services without stirring up the public by raising taxes.

When most people think of inflation they think only of rising prices of widely-used commodities and products: energy, food, housing. This is backward. Rising prices don't cause inflation, they are a symptom of the excess printing of money. As more money gets created out of nothing and the new dollars are not spent on new goods and services, the value of each dollar in circulation declines, and prices are raised to make up the difference.

> **As more money gets created out of nothing and the new dollars are not spent on new goods and services, the value of each dollar in circulation declines, and prices are raised to make up the difference.**

That's why when making investment decisions I have always kept an eye on Federal Reserve statistics that show the supply of money in the economy. When it's going up at a faster rate, you can bet inflation is not far behind. When it goes sideways or down over a period of time, deflation might be on the horizon.

Selling by Emotion

Sales people working in the financial industry take advantage of the innocence of most people by appealing to their fear and greed. All too often their sales pitches are fashioned around how their products and services will make you feel good and safe.

In the year or so after the attacks of September 11, 2001, investors were fearful and the investment industry sales people were pushing so-called "guaranteed" investment products that were guaranteed to restrict your ability to make money, and their ability to enhance theirs. These were "feel-good" products, with sales pitches designed to encourage clients to buy them because it would make them feel more comfortable.

My job is not to make clients feel good. It is to teach the truth about how money works. This often makes clients uncomfortable, which is exactly what I want. I want them to understand that when you get too comfortable, you tend to make decisions for the wrong reasons.

When Money Talks, The Truth is Silent

When Paul Volcker became head of the Federal Reserve in 1979, he said, in essence, "We were wrong and we cannot continue to do what we have been," which was attempting to manage the economy by raising interest rates to slow inflation, and lowering them to spur growth.

Volcker reversed policy from managing interest rates to managing the quantity of money in a long-term, non-inflationary way. But I didn't believe a word of it because it seemed the previous Fed chairmen had lied repeatedly.

Within 18 months, I started believing that Volcker was going to follow through and actually reduce the money supply, which would bring down the very high interest rates we had, which would in turn reduce the cost of capital and improve corporate balance sheets. That would be good for stocks.

In the spring of 1981, with the Dow Jones Industrials trading between 800 and 1,000 (a high it had not pierced in about a dozen years), I began to tell audiences that interest rates were going to start a declining trend. I made a conservative prediction that within the next ten years there was a good chance that the Dow could reach 3,000.

Like they did with my gold move, my ex-colleagues made fun of me, the crazy guy who was saying the Dow Industrials would triple in less than a decade. This was at a time when the economy was really struggling, and the press was full of gloom and doom. Most "experts" claimed the Dow would never stay above 1,000. The Dow broke through 3,000 in the summer of 1990.

> My ex-colleagues made fun of me, the crazy guy who was saying the Dow Industrials would triple in less than a decade. The Dow broke through 3,000 in the summer of 1990.

The betrayal of the Federal Reserve continues to this day. In 2005, the media reported that the Fed was being tight with the money supply. But I watch what they do, not listen to what they say. In reality, the Fed was increasing the money supply, growing it like crazy. Those who saw the real economic numbers knew that a booming economy was underway. We ended up with a bull market, housing boom (and bust), and a great deal of speculation.

What It Means for the Future

When making investment decisions to build and maintain wealth, a steward of money like myself must keep in mind that monetary and fiscal policy decisions are driven by governments all over the world. They make the rules and can change them whenever they choose. There is no way for you and me to know what they are going to do next.

But there is one constant that can keep us protected in case their next move brings down our financial system: Do not have any long-term investments that are claims on paper money. Instead, listen to history and diversify your investments among ownership positions. Then hedge your ownership with real money—the kind governments cannot control and manipulate: gold. I tell my clients that I hope they never make a nickel on their gold and gold-mining investments because if they do, it likely means something wrong is happening in the world. Gold is like insurance: you buy it hoping you never need it.

As long as the U.S. Dollar is accepted as a legitimate form of money, a gold hedge may hold down the returns of your ownership investments in the short term. But I am glad to give up a little return for real world safety and piece of mind.

Sometime in the future, people will wake up to find that our monetary house of cards has collapsed and the U.S. Dollar will be added to the list of history's dead currencies. The well-man-

> **Sometime in the future, people will wake up to find that our monetary house of cards has collapsed and the U.S. Dollar will be added to the list of history's dead currencies.**

aged companies of the world will still be there and hopefully you will own shares in them. Your gold hedge, in addition to skyrocketing in value, will provide you buying power until the government comes out with a new money.

I hope you never experience this disaster scenario in your lifetime but just in case you forgot, my family did, in Europe. My family and I have lived through the unthinkable and I intend to stay prepared for the next time, which will inevitably one day arrive.

If you know the past, you can prepare for the future.

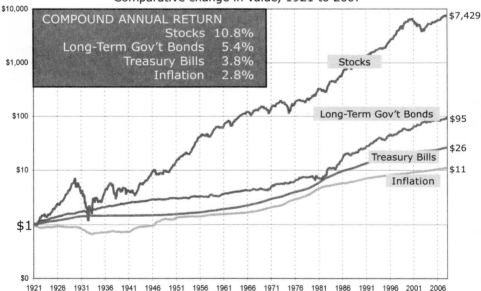

Stocks, Bonds, Bills, and Inflation
Comparative change in value, 1921 to 2007

COMPOUND ANNUAL RETURN

Stocks	10.8%
Long-Term Gov't Bonds	5.4%
Treasury Bills	3.8%
Inflation	2.8%

Stocks — $7,429
Long-Term Gov't Bonds — $95
Treasury Bills — $26
Inflation — $11

Hypothetical value of $1 invested at the beginning of 1921. Assumes reinvestment of income and no transaction costs or taxes. This data is for illustrative purposes only and not indicative of any investment. An investment cannot be made directly in an index. Past performance is no guarantee of future results.
Sources—Stocks: Standard and Poor's 500, an unmanaged group of securities considered representative of the stock market in general; Long-Term Government Bonds: 10-year U.S. Government Bond; Treasury Bills–30-day U.S. Treasury Bill; Inflation–Consumer Price Index. Stock, Long-Term Government Bond, and Treasury Bill data prepared using Global Financial Data. (Find a printable version online at www.ManarinOnMoney.com)

Redefining Risk

The three wealth-building lessons I hope you've learned thus far all have to do with controlling risk. This is an important aspect of investing that most people get wrong. At one end of the spectrum, there are those who think putting money in the FDIC-insured bank is avoiding risk. But that's actually a risky thing to do because chances are good that inflation and taxes will cause you to fall behind instead of getting ahead.

At the other end of the spectrum, there are those who go gunning for the big score: like my father holding on to the cobalt mine stock until he'd squandered a $40,000 profit, or all those Enron employees holding out for $135 a share.

The three risk-controlling lessons are:

○ **Don't hurry to pay down your mortgage—** Using extra money to accelerate paying down the principal on the mortgage on your residence is almost always the worst use of cash, as many people discovered in 2007 when home prices took a nose-dive. Ironically, it is those who owned their homes free and clear who may have lost the most. If they'd put that money in a diversified portfolio of stock mutual funds, they could have made a big profit while the housing market was tanking. One does not "build equity" by paying back the bank. Instead, you lock away precious dollars that under most circumstances could be earning more money elsewhere, and be more accessible in an emergency.

○ **Strive to be an owner, not a lender.** Bank CDs, insurance contracts, bonds and other guaranteed-return investments make you a lender, which robs you of the chance to participate in the growth of the economies of the world.

○ **Insure yourself against economic calamity** with gold-related investments, and hope to God you never make money on them.

Once you've got the risk control concept under your belt, you can move on to how to reap the rewards of intelligent, common sense investing.

MANARIN ON MONEY

5

Spread The Wealth

THE NEXT TIME your head is turned by the new, new thing in investments, consider where we are in history. It's been five thousand or so years since the ancient cultures of the world emerged and began inventing the concepts and mechanics of value, money, and trade. Somewhere someone had to figure out how many goats equaled one cow, and how many dried fish it would take to buy a gourd-full of rice.

Two thousand years ago, merchants in the Middle East had to figure out a way to finance goods being carried all the way to India. It was costly and risky to wait as long as it took for a camel caravan to cross the deserts and return with payment. A lot could go wrong along the way. So a pay-now, deliver-later system evolved. It became institutionalized during the eighteenth century to finance the growing international trade in rice and cotton, and really caught on in the U.S. after the Civil War. Today we call these futures contracts.

Until the late 1700s, when some French scientists invented the metric system, the same weight of potatoes could be calculated dozens of ways depending on which region or town of the country you happened to be in. Pricing was guess-work, and measuring distance or the size of a piece of land was done by stepping it off, or some similar crude method.

In the context of the financial past, the eight decades that have elapsed since the Roaring 1920s turned into the Great Depression have been a ripple in time. Yet if you watch enough business television programming, and read enough web sites, magazines, and newspapers, you'd think that there are all sorts of riddles and mysteries about money that are being discovered all the time. We're being shouted at by a mob of experts, talking heads, and frantic messages urging us to "Act now, or you'll miss out!"

> **We're being shouted at by a mob of experts, talking heads, and frantic messages urging us to 'Act now, or you'll miss out!'**

There is no mystery at all. It's simple common sense, and that common sense has been around for some time. Wealth is created through a combination of ownership and time. Added to that is diversification, a relatively recent concept in the history of money.

The idea that stocks outperform bonds, for example, was first popularized in 1924 in a small book entitled "Common Stocks as Long Term Investments," by Edgar Lawrence Smith. Smith did extensive research that proved a diversified portfolio of stocks always outperformed bonds over the long run, a con-clusion that was considered so revolutionary at the time that the book took five years to catch on, just before the Crash of 1929. The same year Smith's book was published, the Massachusetts Investors Trust, the first open-end mutual fund in the world, began business.

Unfortunately, the Federal Reserve had printed so much money that the whole country had gone stock crazy, thanks to the brokerage houses making it easy to invest with borrowed money. Smart people saw the Crash coming and got out of the way. Economist Roger Babson (who founded a business school) and wealthy financier Bernard Baruch were two who famously predicted and therefore profited from the Crash of 1929.

Just as in 1999, in 1929 the rest of the investing public ignored these warnings and some "experts" made fools of themselves by being completely wrong. One of the most quoted is Irving Fisher, a Yale economist, who said two weeks before the crash, "Stock prices have reached what looks like a permanently high plateau. I do not feel there will soon be, if ever, a 50 or 60 point break below present levels."

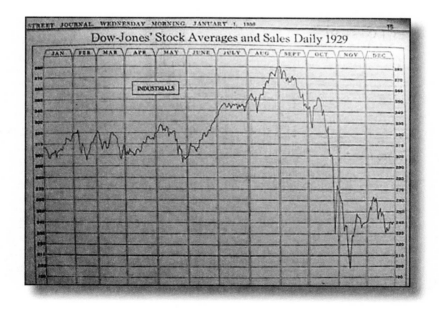

The Templeton Touch

Ten years after the Crash of 1929, with the news of Hitler's invasion of Poland, a young man working for a seismic exploration company in New York went to his boss and asked to borrow $10,000 to invest in the stock market. His boss listened to the young man's argument that the coming war in Europe would bring an end to the Depression and introduce a period of high economic activity. He agreed to lend the money.

> Templeton once joked, 'I have put (my) philosophies into a simple statement: Help people. When people are desperately trying to sell, help them and buy. When people are enthusiastically trying to buy, help them and sell.'

The young man, who had worked years earlier for a stock brokerage, went to a former colleague and put in orders to buy 100 shares of every stock on the New York exchange that was trading at $1 a share or less. About a third of them were insolvent, and thus very cheap. The broker tried to talk him out of it but the young man was determined.

Before the war ended, he sold his motley $10,000 collection of stocks for the princely sum of $40,000 (equal in buying power to about $600,000 in 2007). Only four of the more than one hundred companies he originally invested in had actually gone out of existence. He had discovered the power of thinking globally, diversifying, and—most important of all—buying when everyone else was selling.

That young man was John Templeton, who managed the

mutual fund I discovered after it had been earning an average of nearly 14 percent a year since its inception in the 1950s. Templeton was a pioneer and he was still pioneering in the 1970s, about the time I persuaded my boss at the brokerage firm I worked for that we should pull equity out of our homes and invest it in Templeton's fund.

Templeton (at left, with me, several years ago) was smart, creative, and had the kind of common sense that has made people like himself and Warren Buffett wealthy while keeping a lid on their risk.

Templeton, who was knighted in 1986 for his philanthropic activities, joked in a 2004 interview, "I have put [my] philosophies into a simple statement: Help people. When people are desperately trying to sell, help them and buy. When people are enthusiastically trying to buy, help them and sell."

This outlook persuaded him to buy Ford Motor Company stock cheap in the late 1970s when everyone else was eager to sell, and then to sell it for a big profit later when everybody wanted to buy. His strategy and objectivity made it possible for him to predict the bull market of the 1990s, the market crash that followed, and—in his 90s now—the bursting of the housing bubble.

These were not hard predictions to make. I know because I've made a string of them myself, and been there to "help" the eager sellers or buyers when they were acting out of fear or greed instead of common sense. In Chapter 7, I list some of the seventeen times I "hocked" the house—borrowed against equity—to earn a higher, low-risk return elsewhere. When you study the series of decisions and how I arrived at them, you'll see why anyone with a basic understanding of how money works, and the courage to act on it, can grow wealth by doing exactly the opposite of what the crowd is doing.

A World of Opportunity

John Templeton has made untold hundreds of millions for himself and his shareholders. He is a visionary and one of his visions I share, because it has worked consistently for my clients and me for all these years, is to diversify globally. Raised on a Tennessee farm, he got himself to Yale and Oxford University and then traveled around the globe. He returned to the States a truly world-wise young man. When he went into the investment business, he expanded his strategy of diversification to include investments in other countries.

A key reason for my success is similar to Templeton's in that I arrived in the US at age ten with a global point of view. Through my own eyes and through the many family stories I heard around the dinner table of how our family survived the worst times in modern history, I grew up with a lot of knowledge about and interest in money. When I discovered John Templeton and learned about his approach to controlling risk and taking advantage of mob psychology, I immediately got it.

"It" is spreading your money around in a strategic way to reduce the risk of having too many eggs in the wrong basket. For the same reason that you shouldn't put all your money in one stock (like Enron), you shouldn't have all your money in currency-based assets. The American dollar may seem like the safest place to keep your investments, and it was for a long time. But no currency is truly safe so long as its government has the power to print money anytime it wants. This was brought home to me during one of the visits I made with my father to Europe, to our old hometown.

No currency is truly safe so long as its government has the power to print money anytime it wants.

We were driving along a winding mountain road in northern Italy one day when my father suddenly pointed to a small house atop a hill. "There was a man back in the old days who lived in that house until they found him frozen to death one day. He had owned a chain of gelato (Italian ice cream) stores and was rich until the Ruhr Crisis came along in 1923.

"The man stopped coming into town and when someone went out to check up on him, they found him stiff as a board, surrounded by boxes filled with worthless German marks. What a way to go!"

I wasn't around in 1923, so I asked my father, "How did our family survive that time?"

"We were marble people," he said. "We didn't understand about what was happening with the money but we knew marble. If a rich guy wanted us to build something for him, we'd take payment in extra marble. For example, if a baron wanted us to build a marble structure and it took a ton of marble to do the job, we would take as payment a second ton of marble that we stored. After the currency collapsed, our cash situation was as bad as everyone else's. But when the dust settled, we had a warehouse full of good marble we could sell. So we came out of it in pretty good shape."

Marble, as it turned out, was almost as good as gold or stocks. It was a tangible asset and my father's family had survived by being owners, not lenders. These are dramatic examples of what happens in the case of extreme economic crisis. Hopefully the U.S. will never face anything quite so cataclysmic. Regardless, the mechanics of money never change. Owning trumps lending.

A Short Course in Inflation

Governments (or the Federal Reserve Bank) that start printing money with nothing to back it up usually never stop. Would you? They are like drug addicts who get hooked on the first high. The only way to break the pattern is to stop, and just like drugs, quitting can be painful.

When governments try to stop printing and rein in the inflation they have caused, the economy suffers a hangover we call a recession or, if it's bad enough, a depression.

To understand how money works when governments abuse it, imagine that you own one of America's thriving businesses. The U.S. Treasury controls the printing of the country's fiat money (paper currency backed up by nothing). When the government needs money to pay the expenses of running the country, or to wage a war, it just prints more.

If it prints enough and spends it building bridges or equipping armies, it starts to spread around to others and they in turn spend it. Your business begins to grow. You decide to take advantage of this economic boom by expanding, hiring more people and building more factories.

Soon businesses everywhere are booming and everything is working out great except that when the supply of money gets out of hand, prices go up, for everyone. Everything you need to run your business is costing more and even though your business is growing, your profits are shrinking. You decide that the answer is to grow bigger, build more factories, hire more people, make more products for an eager market.

But unlike the government, you don't have a printing press to make more money. You have to go and borrow from the bank, which is in turn borrowing the money to lend you from the government, whose printing press has been running three shifts a day to keep up.

Finally, inflation becomes so bad and people are complaining so loudly that the government decides it finally has to do something. So it stops the presses. No more new money goes into the economy, which government economists hope will stop the inflation. But the economy has gotten hooked on the cycle of growing money, better wages, higher prices, and being able to borrow easily. Now money is scarce and expensive to borrow, growth slows, and the economy begins to stagnate along with your business.

This forces you to lay off employees and sell some of your business assets to keep up with those loans you took out. Other businesses are also letting people go and losing money. The country develops a bad hangover, or possibly something worse.

The Depression of the 1930s was caused by just such a scenario. The villain was the Federal Reserve which printed a lot of money during the 1920s. They did it in response to demand, without regard to consequences. Roy Young, a Federal Reserve governor, is reported to have said in 1928, "I am laughing at myself sitting here and trying to keep 125 million people from doing what they want to do." What they wanted to do was buy stocks and get rich quick.

This should sound familiar to you. Just as during the 1920s, during the 1990s a lot of the money flowing into the stock market was purchased with money borrowed against rising stock prices. The higher the stock market soared, the more money people could borrow to buy still more stock. It's a great way to make money without having to put up cash—when the stock market is bullish and rising. The problem comes when the last buyers have arrived at the party, and there's no one left to sell to.

When prices fall as fast as they did in 2000, those who bought stock with borrowed money—on margin—had to pay back the loans. But no one likes to put up cash just to hold on to a stock that's falling, so suddenly all the buyers become sellers and prices collapse. This is a result not of bad investing but rank speculation. When people express suspicion that the stock market is just a big gambling pit, this is the kind of activity they're talking about—taking huge risks to try to game the system.

> **"The guilt for the Depression must be lifted from the shoulders of the free market economy, and placed where it properly belongs: at the doors of politicians, bureaucrats, and the mass of 'enlightened' economists."**

If we have another economic collapse, we will know who to thank. As economist and author Murray Rothbard states in his book "America's Great Depression," "The guilt for the Great Depression must, at long last, be lifted from the shoulders of the free market economy, and placed where it properly belongs: at the doors of politicians, bureaucrats, and the mass of 'enlightened' economists. And in any other depression, past or future, the story will be the same."

One Final History Lesson

Incredibly, the Great Depression that the Federal Reserve made possible made the Federal Reserve more powerful. In 1932, using its totalitarian authority over our money and banking system, Congress passed a law known as the Glass-Steagall Act that gave the Fed permission to use not only commercial bills and gold, but also government securities, as collateral for Federal Reserve Notes.

A government security, such as a Treasury bond, is an IOU. So this would be like showing up at a bank with all your debts, and trying to use them as collateral for a loan. If you or I tried to do that, we might be arrested for bank fraud. But the Federal Reserve System has that power and, in the process, they can multiply the money supply many times over, a process known as monetizing debt.

When Roosevelt ordered citizens to surrender their gold assets and devalued the currency by 69 percent, it was the economic equivalent of your doctor draining you of 69 percent of your blood. Our economy was sick and FDR made it worse.

By the late 1930s, the winds of war were blowing again and the Glass-Steagall act made it easy for the U.S. Government to pay for our participation in World War II with all those extra dollars, which created more inflation. This has been the pattern for every war since.

The Fed printed more and more fiat money with no gold backing, but foreign banks could still redeem dollars from the U.S. government at $35 an ounce. Over time, this depleted our nation's gold reserves until Richard Nixon closed the gold window on the world in 1971.

For the first time in the history of America, the dollar was a pure fiat paper money. If you or I tried to pull what the

U.S. Government did in 1971, we would be declared bankrupt.

If you tried to pull what the Government did in 1971, you would be declared bankrupt.

The final insult came in 1980, when Congress passed the Monetary Control Act, allowing all state, local, and foreign debt to be accepted as collateral for our money. That means, in effect, that banks can now lend all the money they want with essentially no tangible assets.

The investment industry has since promoted the idea that investments like CDs, fixed annuities, and bonds—claims on paper money—are safe when they are in fact dangerous because you lose buying power, either through inflation or more quickly if the dollar collapses.

If you were confused about what was called the subprime mortgage meltdown in 2007, you should now begin to understand the mess created by the Federal Reserve and our friends in Congress. It may be politically crafty to point the finger at the mortgage companies and Wall Street—they bear some responsibility—but the real villain is bad government policy.

My goal in this chapter has been to explain in the simplest way possible the reason why growing and preserving wealth comes from owning real assets, not from anything that is dependent on the perceived value of paper money, which isn't worth the paper it's printed on.

6

Fear Factors

"It is a curious fact that capital is generally most fearful when prices...are low and safe, and boldest at the heights when there is danger."

—Legendary investor Bernard M. Baruch

ONE OF THE most important discussions I have with new clients goes something like this: At some point, you will wake up and be horrified to discover that the financial markets have flown into an air pocket and the value of your portfolio has taken a big hit. This will cause your adrenal gland to go into high gear and your heart will pound with fear.

Fear is a natural reaction, but not part of a successful investment strategy. We try to prepare investors for the inevitable—nobody's right all the time, and no investment goes straight up. It's part of my role in the lives of my clients to train them how to be patient investors, to resist the urge to act in panic.

Anywhere you park your money or other assets involves some degree of risk. When it comes to our homes, we can manage that risk by carrying insurance against fire and other calamities. But we cannot eliminate risk altogether, as many people dis-

> **Every decision has risk, even cash sitting in the bank. There's risk of the dollar collapsing, and the insidious risk of inflation. Every day your money loses buying power.**

covered when the real estate market collapsed. How many times have you heard the old saw, "Real estate never goes down"? Never turns out to be sometimes, especially in places like California where prices have in the past fallen as much as 40 percent.

Every decision has risk, even cash sitting in a bank. There's risk of the dollar collapsing, and the insidious risk of inflation. Every day your money loses buying power.

The stock market has its own mythology: stocks earn on average about 10 percent a year. This one is even less true than the one that says real estate values never decline. It is accurate that over decades of time, the average annual return from investing in stocks has been about 10 percent. But along the way we have gone through periods when the stock market falls apart, as it did in 2000 through 2002 after the technology bubble of the 1990s.

Whether you made your tidy 10 percent a year will depend on when you bought and when you sold. You might have lost 50 percent, or you may have earned 100 percent. Out of nearly 60 possible 20-year "slices" of the stock market that have elapsed since the Crash of 1929 (as in, you bought the Dow Jones Industrial Average and held it for any continuous block of 20 years), your average rate of return could have been as low as 3 percent and as high as 18 percent.

If you happened to hit the overall average of 10 percent a year, a $100,000 initial investment would have grown in 20 years to about $675,000. If you were unlucky and caught the low-end slice, you'd only have $185,000, and at the high end you'd have as much as $2.7 million. This is before the erosion of inflation and the cost of taxes, so on the low end you not only would have failed to make any progress in the buying power of your dollars, you'd have lost some.

In the real world, people have financial crises, health issues, and become susceptible during anxious times to the investment industry's sales pitches. In the real world, the statistics are quite dismal.

Few people actually hold on to an investment for two decades, which makes the 10-percent-a-year pitch even less relevant to real-life investors. In the real world, people have financial crises, health issues, and become susceptible during anxious times to the investment industry's sales pitches. In the real world, the statistics are quite dismal.

If you had been patient and calm between 1986 and 2005, your average return of the S&P 500 index would have been 11.90 percent. But according to Dalbar Inc., a leading financial-services research firm, the average actual returns of investors over the same time was a paltry 3.9 percent. Dalbar reported that the difference was caused by investors' emotions driving their choices—selling after prices had already fallen and buying after they'd risen.

Another study entitled "Dumb Money," conducted by professors at Yale and the University of Chicago, found that between 1983 and 2003, the hottest mutual funds—those experiencing the greatest inflows of money—performed much worse than mutual funds that investors were dumping.

Left to their own devices, most people are inclined to follow the crowd—even off a cliff.

It's Always Scary Times

I advise my clients to take a deep breath and remember that there is always something to worry about, and that the secret to success is often to do exactly the opposite of what your adrenal gland is urging you to do.

There's always something to be frightened about. In 2007, home prices fell, oil prices soared, credit became tight, and the stock market was exceptionally volatile. As I always do, I advised my clients to take a deep breath and remember that there is always something to worry about, and that the secret to success is often to do exactly the opposite of what your adrenal gland is urging you to do.

As John Templeton observed, the time to be greedy is when others are afraid, and the time to be afraid is when others are greedy. This is hard to do, but once you've internalized it, you'll be making money while others are counting losses.

Our evolutionary instincts—safety in numbers—is what the Wall Street establishment and the media counts on to make their living: creating excitement and anxiety that keeps us tuned in and susceptible to persuasion. This desire to be among the majority is apparently baked in to our DNA.

Solomon Asch, a pioneer of social psychology, did a number of experiments that proved that people could be persuaded to believe what their eyes knew couldn't be true. In one, he drew two lines on a blackboard that were of different lengths. Then he recruited a group of people who were instructed to say, regardless of what they saw or what anyone told them, that the two lines were actually of equal length.

Then he brought in the guinea pig subjects and asked them to say whether the lines were equal or not. Two thirds of the subjects allowed themselves to be persuaded by the majority that the lines were equal, even though they clearly were not.

This phenomenon goes a long way toward explaining why most people have so much trouble managing their money. We're bombarded with twenty-four-hour-a-day business and financial news online, on television, in the print media, and in our mailboxes, reminding us of all the horrors and hot opportunities awaiting us around the next corner. Much of what is served up as business and personal finance news is warmed over and juiced up to grab your attention, but does little to inform, and nothing to make you money.

For example, if you lived in San Francisco on September 1, 1998, around the time of another major financial crisis, your morning coffee would have been accompanied by this headline in the *San Francisco Chronicle:* "PANIC HAMMERS MARKET". Above the headline were eleven red, downward-pointing arrows showing the bloodbath in selected stocks and indices. Below the headline was a photograph of a trader standing at his desk and holding his head in his hands. Scary times! This headline no doubt convinced some people to call their advisors and sell everything.

But on your way home from work, if you had picked up a copy of the afternoon San Francisco Examiner, you'd have found an equally huge headline: "STOCKS BOUNCE BACK, Dow up second-biggest point gain ever." Happy days are here again!

Don't Just Stand There

In times of volatility, people lose confidence in their judgment and become paralyzed.

In times of volatility, people lose confidence in their judgment and become paralyzed, rationalizing that the smartest move is to sit on their hands and wait for things to settle down. That may seem safe but history shows that doing nothing is the second costliest mistake you can make during a market meltdown, right behind selling at the bottom.

A long term chart of the Dow Jones Industrial Average illustrates this. The Dow crashed by a historical percentage in October 1987, but had completely recovered within two years and went on to new highs. It crashed again in 1998, recovered in less than a year, and went on to new highs. It crashed in 2002, recovered in two years, then marched to a new high in 2007.

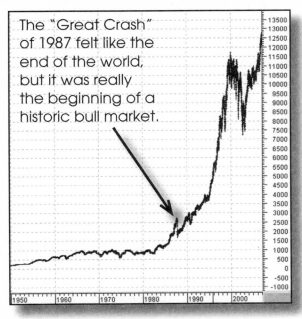

The "Great Crash" of 1987 felt like the end of the world, but it was really the beginning of a historic bull market.

For the long term investor, this periodic volatility and fear are at worst irrelevant. Periods of high anxiety in the markets are to me what panic in a wildebeest herd is to a stalking lion—a good time to pick off an easy meal.

It's important to distinguish between taking advantage of mob behavior (greed or fear), and trying to anticipate broad market trends, the thoroughly discredited practice of trying to "time the market," guessing whether we're in a bull or bear phase. Volatility can be your friend in good times or bad. All that matters is whether it is an opportunity to buy good assets low and the chance to sell them when they get high. In this case, one of the riskiest things you can do is to let the easy prey get away.

One of the dumbest things people do is sell after a plunge because they are terrified of "losing" more. But you don't lose on an investment until you sell, so these people are making their nightmares come true. There are many examples of investments that plunged in price but rebounded and went on to new highs. That's why we counsel people up front: expect the unexpected and ignore it when it happens.

In the 1990 bear market, I had a client that bailed out of the stock market because emotionally he couldn't take the anxiety of watching his portfolio shrink. This client had a significant account that, in spite of my advice, he sold as close to the bottom as you could get. He took the money and bought

> **One of the dumbest things people do is sell after a plunge because they are terrified of "losing" more. But you don't lose on an investment until you sell, so these people are making their nightmares come true.**

an insurance annuity, thinking it was the least risky thing he could do.

I believe annuities are a terrible investment (see Chapter 9), and in this client's case it was an especially costly mistake. During the six or so years that followed, he had earned a total, at most, of 20 percent—a poor return on an annualized basis. Had he stuck to his guns and held on to his investments, he likely would have doubled his money.

Gold Rules

Earlier I talked about how, in the late 1970s, I loaded up on gold-related investments after it became clear to me that President Carter was setting the stage for high inflation. That was an unusual time in that gold was a good investment. But it is always part of my strategy to have some money invested in gold-related assets as insurance against disaster.

The price of gold tends to rise and fall depending on the world's faith in the dollar. When the price of gold rises, it is gaining back buying power in relation to the falling dollar. That's what happened in 2007 when the dollar was collapsing and gold was hitting new highs. Gold is protection against governments that are big printers and spenders of paper money.

It's interesting to note that there is no country in the world today with a gold-backed currency. Russia or South Africa could do it because they have a lot of gold mines. If they did, theirs would be the strongest currencies on the planet.

Bureaucrats reject going back on the gold standard because they want to control the quantity

During a major financial crisis, the golden rule is, "Whoever owns the gold, makes the rules."

of available money. You can't print more gold but you can create paper money from nothing, and that is a cheaper and sneakier way to tax without raising taxes. When a government artificially increases the money in circulation by 10 percent, it has the same effect as taking 10 percent of the public's saving through taxation. Printing more money dilutes the value of the money that's already in circulation. In any other endeavor, this would be called fraud. When governments do it, it's called economic policy.

In case you think this is a minor problem, consider that every major war waged in modern history was financed by printing paper money without gold backing. Ferdinand Lips, a Swiss banker and author, has persuasively argued in recent years that there

> **Every war in modern history was financed by printing paper money without gold backing. Wars would be shorter, if governments returned to gold-based currencies.**

would be less war, and wars would be shorter, if governments were to return to gold-based currencies.

"World history proves that there is a close relationship between monetary systems and war and peace," Lips told a conference in 2002. "It is not widely known that the 19th century was a period of prosperity and economic growth without inflation. It strikes us like a fairytale when we discover that in those days the most important currencies were stable over a long period. The French franc, for example, remained solid for one hundred years. It was the era of the gold standard."

A simple way to protect yourself against the bad behavior of governments and total disaster is to buy gold bullion coins. (Not collectible coins which are marked up above the actual value of the gold. It's also a good idea to shop around to get the best quote.)

Keep your coins at home because if the dollar ever collapses, you may be unable to get to your safety-deposit box. You're better off burying them under your favorite rose bush where you'll know where to find them. If this sounds crazy to you, it's because you never experienced true financial chaos like my family did, and you didn't have the experience of escaping disaster because you owned physical gold.

People often ask me how much gold they should own for their stash. In today's world, $5,000 worth of tenth-ounce gold coins is enough for me to sleep well at night. If our financial house of cards should ever collapse and government currency truly becomes worthless, we will be living in a barter economy, much as my family did when they took marble in payment for their work. During a major financial crisis, the golden rule is, "Whoever owns the gold, makes the rules."

In investment portfolios, I own gold through mutual funds that invest in the common stock of gold-mining companies, which provides an additional layer of safety. I advise against investing in individual gold-mining stocks because, unless you are a geologist, you won't be able to tell the difference between a real gold mine and a hole in the ground with a liar on top.

As with gold bullion coins, I hope I never make money with my gold-mining shares, much as I pay my homeowner or auto insurance premiums hoping I never collect. The purpose of gold-mining shares is to protect the ownership positions in your portfolio from the worst of times.

How much of your assets to keep in gold? I typically aim for 5-7 percent of my portfolio. Periodically, as the values of the rest of my portfolio change, the percentage in gold will drop and I'll buy more until I'm back at 5-7 percent.

Conversely, if the price of gold rises and the percentage of gold assets in my portfolio exceeds my target range, I sell down. As I write this, I have about 7 percent of my portfolio in gold-mining shares.

Getting Gold-Bugged

Those of us who understand the way money works and use gold as a buffer against calamity are often regarded with skepticism. Just as in the late 1970s, around 2000—when gold was setting record lows—my colleagues in the investment world and the media ridiculed me for loading up on gold investments. The media wrote about people like me as "gold bugs," as though we were a bunch of wild-eyed survivalists and hucksters.

The more I was criticized in the press, the more gold assets I bought. To me the negative coverage was as sure as sign as any that gold was cheap, and the shares of gold-mining companies were even cheaper historically.

By 2007, gold-mining shares had risen by 500 percent and more, and then the business writers and the callers into my office changed their tune, asking me if it was a good time to buy gold. It is a ceaseless wonder how so many otherwise intelligent people can get something so basic so wrong with such consistency.

> When the Fed is printing more money, there cannot be any deflation. There can only be inflation, which means interest rates will likely rise and the price of bonds will fall.

The Real Reason to Own Bonds

U.S. Treasury bonds are the most familiar form of investment "insurance." The conventional wisdom is the tired old formula you hear everywhere you turn: a set percent of your money should be in "safe" bonds. When you're in the business of selling investment "products" instead of helping people avoid risk and create wealth, the 60-40, stocks-to-bonds mythology is a quick way of getting a sale. People want simple answers but they end up paying a price for them.

Bonds are a form of insurance, but instead of protecting from inflation, bonds protect from the threat of deflation when interest rates decline and the price of the Treasury bonds increase.

For example, in 1987 there was a threat of a deflationary collapse due to Alan Greenspan's tightening of the money supply to slow inflation. At that time I put 10 percent of our portfolios into long-term U.S. Treasury bond strips (zero coupon bonds whose prices move fastest with charges in interest rates) which rise in value as interest rates decline (deflationary hedge). What followed was a huge crisis and scandal in the banking world that wiped out a whole industry—savings and loan banks—cost the taxpayers a fortune, and drove down the real estate market.

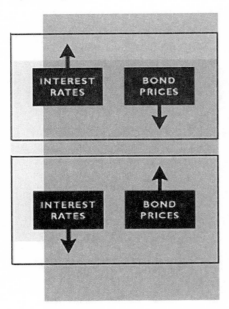

In 1994, there was a spike in interest rates—driving down the price of bonds. It was an opportunity to buy more, which I did. The 1990s were not technically deflationary, but the cost of many essentials declined: oil fell from a Gulf War high of about $40 a barrel to as low as $10 a barrel in 1998; labor costs declined as manufacturing and call centers moved abroad; and technology was producing productivity gains unheard of since the Industrial Revolution.

In the fall of 1998 we experienced a global financial crisis, referred to as the Long Term Capital debacle for the hedge fund at the center of it. The media was promoting fears of a major recession, using as the news hook that the sixtieth anniversary of the Crash of 1929 was just around the corner. It made no sense but it did make for great headlines: "Unhappy 60th Anniversary: Could The Great Depression Happen Again?"

Interest rates briefly plunged as people began buying up Treasury bonds for their perceived safety and drove up the price of bonds. Our portfolios had a nice profit over the cost of the bonds we'd bought earlier.

While the herd was rushing in one direction, the economy was headed the other way. The Fed was printing money to spend its way out of the Long Term Capital crisis, just as they would years later in 2007 with the subprime mortgage crisis.

When the Fed is printing more money, there cannot be any deflation. There can only be inflation, which means interest rates will likely rise and the price of bonds will fall. So in the fall of 1998, I sold all the Treasury bonds in my private mutual funds that I managed for a handsome profit, have not bought any since, and won't until I can establish to my satisfaction that the Fed is trying to rein in the supply of money and create the risk of deflation. Don't hold your breath.

Defining Financial Safety

Suppose your investment advisor called you up one day and said, "I want to recommend a stock to you. I admit that its performance record hasn't been the best. It started trading at $100 in 1913. By 1953 it had dropped to about $30 a share and by 1977 to about $15 a share. Today it trades around $4, and I predict it will lose much more in the future. How many shares do you want to buy?"

"None!" you shout. But that's what people do every day. This investment that's lost over 95 percent of its value in nearly a century is American money. The U.S. dollar of 1913 would have the buying power today of four cents. Where did the other 96 cents go? It was eaten up by the rising cost of living, averaging 3 percent a year, a cost caused by the Federal Reserve System.

In spite of this dismal record, the financial industry continues to offer investments tied to the dollar, arguing that the return is "guaranteed and safe," in some cases by the same government that caused the inflation. Based on the history of the dollar and our current economic environment, the only guarantee offered by government currency is the steady, unrelenting loss of buying power.

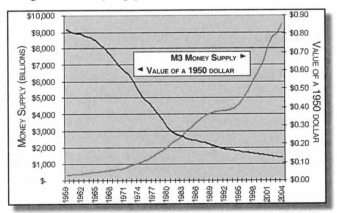

The eroding effect on the value of a dollar (descending line) as the Fed increased the quantity of money by printing more.

The Big Picture

When you put together an investment portfolio that takes into account all that I've described thus far, you have what I call a diversified ownership portfolio. The philosophy behind the portfolio model is that the future is unpredictable but risk can be controlled so you'll be able to weather almost any storm.

In a given year some parts of the puzzle will outperform others. But collectively, over time, the portfolio will yo-yo up a flight of stairs—in Wall Street parlance, climbing a "wall of worry."

After thirty years of studying money, economics, and the investment markets, I am still fine-tuning my approach. But the basic rules will always apply, although the details and the chatter are always changing.

This is not a how-to book but I hope to throw some light on how-does, as in, "How does money work and grow?" If the answer was obvious, we would not be a nation of confused and anxious investors making foolish choices with their financial futures.

Whether you are a self-directed investor, an investor in search of an advisor, an investor who is paralyzed by fear or blinded by greed, or an investor who feels he or she isn't getting straight answers or helpful advice, the more you know about how things really work, the better your decisions are likely to be, and the sooner you'll be able to establish a path to reach your goals.

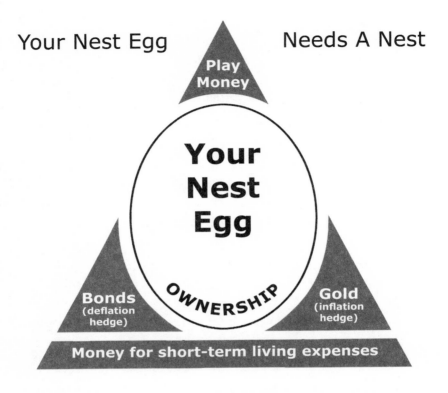

Your Nest Egg Needs A Nest

Play Money

Your Nest Egg

Bonds (deflation hedge)

OWNERSHIP

Gold (inflation hedge)

Money for short-term living expenses

The model I use to teach investors how to manage money is to think of your nest egg as the bulk of your wealth, which should be invested in long-term ownership positions, such as mutual funds invested only in stocks.

Your nest egg rests on a small portion of 30-year U.S. Treasury bonds that tend to do better when we have deflation, as happened during the Great Depression; and a small portion of money in gold-mining shares, which tend to do best during times of high inflation, as happened in the late 1970s.

Finally, set aside enough money for short-term living expenses.

You can top it all off with any extra funds you want to set aside for indulgences—"play" money.

7

When Opportunity Knocks

> **Money is like a sixth sense without which you cannot make a complete use of the other five.**
>
> —W. Somerset Maugham,
> from "Of Human Bondage"

O NE OF THE easy choices the investment industry promotes to get people to buy investment products is the notion that your investments should reflect your "risk profile"— your tolerance for market ups and downs. If you're young, you're supposed to be able to tolerate more risk because you aren't going to need the money for a long time and will be able to ride out the market's swings.

If you're older, the theory goes that you should avoid volatile investments so you don't get caught short right when you need the money.

There are elements of truth in these ideas but asking an investor to self-evaluate his or her tolerance for risk is for most people like asking them to perform surgery on themselves. Unless you're a professional or a lifelong student of investing, you have no basis on which to judge the relative risk of a particular investment, nor to predict the unpredictable future. The

Risk is less about volatility and more about your money losing buying power.

experts can't do it. How could you?

Fearing the unknown, most will declare themselves averse to risk, which may in fact be a risky choice. I don't worry about short-term volatility because when you are a buyer in a mob of sellers, prices fall to bargain levels and most of the risk has already been squeezed out.

That's what happened with oil and gold between 1998 and 2000. At $10 a barrel, when adjusted for inflation, oil was as affordable as it had been a hundred years earlier. At $280 an ounce, when adjusted for inflation, gold hadn't been as cheap in more than a quarter-century.

Buying these sorts of assets requires no special knowledge to understand that the risk of your investment going down is very small. Gold is finite and unlikely to suddenly be in great supply, and you only had to look around you to see that the world was continuing to chug along on oil, using more every year.

For long-term investors, risk is less about short term volatility and more about your money losing buying power.

A Short History Lesson

In some ways, the American economy has been on a long upswing for twenty-five years, starting in 1982. That's when a bull market started that drove the Dow Jones Industrial Average from a low of just under 800 to a recent high above 14,000.

All along the way, there was doom and gloom, good years and bad, but on average the Dow rose about 12 percent a year.

It's helpful to remember this when fear paralyzes your ability to act. There will always be a reason to do nothing, and plenty of noise to keep you confused and anxious.

Every year there has been some new drum-beat of doom. Here is the dismal-sounding march of time, during which more wealth was created for more people than at any time in history.

Always A Reason Not To Invest

1977: Market Slumps
1978: Interest Rates Spike
1979: Oil Prices Skyrocket
1980: Interest Rates Hit All-Time Highs
1981: Steep Recession Begins
1982: Worst Recession in 40 Years
1983: Market Hits Unsustainable High
1984: Record Federal Deficits
1985: Economic Growth Slows
1986: Dow Nears 2000—Unsustainable!
1987: Black Tuesday—Dow Drops 500 Points
1988: Fraud Destroys Thrifts, $500 Billion Bailout
1989: 8 Year Economic Boom Comes To A Halt
1990: Gulf War, Oil Price Spike
1991: U.S. Economy Falls Into A Recession
1992: Major Job Slump
1993: Income Tax Hikes; Health Care Debacle
1994: NAFTA Raises Globalization Fears
1995: Oklahoma City Bombing
1996: Dow Rises 25%, Prices Unsustainable
1997: Asian Financial Crisis
1998: Clinton Impeachment, Kosovo War

1999: Wall Street Fever, Greed Everywhere
2000: Tech Bubble Bursts, Stock Markets Fall
2001: 9/11 Terrorist Attacks, Markets Crash
2002: Recession Sinks US Economy
2003: Iraq War; Corporate, Wall Street Frauds
2004: Exporting Jobs, Real Estate Fever
2005: Hurricane Katrina, Oil Spikes
2006: Housing Overheats, China Owns US
2007: Subprime Meltdown, Real Estate Collapse

The lesson I draw from all this is that I hope the next 30 years are as terrible as the last because, if they are, we'll all be better off.

Going All In

Clients who have stayed with me over the years eventually get the message and develop a higher tolerance for volatility than they had when I met them. I urge my clients to be nearly 100 percent in equities at all times no matter their age. This means that when we hit a bear market, as we did in the 2000 to 2002 period, their portfolios fall.

But instead of getting scared, many of my clients understood that this was an opportunity to substantially increase their wealth by borrowing and buying more mutual fund shares at bargain prices. When the market eventually rose again—as it always does—those who seized this opportunity were rewarded with handsome profits.

The next time the stock market takes a dive and you hear people complaining or worrying, you should be one of the very few who says, "Oh, this is a wonderful opportunity. The market's on sale!" What you say and how you react to situations like these may very well determine what level of financial prosperity you experience years from now.

This is the principle I try to get my clients and radio listeners to focus on: all the degrees and technical studies in the world cannot beat good old common sense. In his excellent 1946 book "Economics in One Lesson," author Henry Hazlitt reminds us, "Economics is haunted by more fallacies than any other study known to man."

So is investing. It is one of those areas where the people giving bad advice often present their errors to the public more effectively than those giving good advice, as evidenced by the blind acceptance of conventional wisdom in the financial media, Wall Street, and on business-book bestseller lists.

The next time the stock market takes a dive and you hear people complaining or worrying, you should be one of the very few who says, 'Oh, this is a wonderful opportunity. The market's on sale!'

The best way to take advantage of conventional wisdom is to do the opposite of what you hear. In my early days as an investor, I learned that by the time you hear about something from the brokerage firms or in the media, most of the money's already been made.

Although my father made a common mistake holding on to his investment in the cobalt mine as it crashed, he had good instincts in many other areas. When I was a child learning to speak English, I became a fan of CBS News anchor Walter Cronkite.

One day I noticed how much bad news Cronkite was reporting and asked my father, "Papa, why is this guy so negative? This is America! Things are good." My father replied, "So, quit listening."

That sounded like good advice and I quit regularly watching the nightly news when I was a teenager. Once I had learned about free-market economics, I realized that the newscasters knew nothing about the financial news they were reporting. I found myself less influenced by negative emotions, focusing instead on the real world around me, and on statistics about what the government was doing with our money.

A metaphor for how a central bank can ruin an economy is how one can ruin a cup of coffee. The coffee is the economy. Interest rates and money supply are the cream and sugar. If you add too much cream and sugar to a cup of coffee, it becomes undrinkable. The same applies to the economy and monetary policy.

So instead of listening to what the policymakers are saying, watch what they are doing.

Different This Time?

Wall Street moves in a herd, which is why so many people get hurt when things go wrong—they follow each other off the cliff. Smart investors think for themselves and ignore advice that is based on the rationalization that "everyone's doing it, so it must be right."

In February 2000, I visited a portfolio manager who ran a fund that specialized in technology stocks. I had invested in his fund in 1996 and the investment was up more than 600 percent. I knew it was time to sell because we'd made a lot of money and technology was beginning to look very overpriced.

As you would expect, the portfolio manager tried to change my mind. He assured me that he was still buying more technology stocks because the future was bright and his companies were going to make a lot of money. I was surprised because he was not a newbie but one who had been around long enough to have lived through major ups and downs. He should have known better but somewhere along the line he'd drunk the Kool-Aid.

> There is no such thing as a "New Economy" or any other tagline or buzzword people may use to suggest that somehow the laws of nature have been repealed. It's never going to be "different this time."

I asked him, "How can you be buying stocks of companies at two hundred-plus times their earnings when historically stock prices are too high at thirty times earnings?"

"This time is different," he promised.

I sold our position in that mutual fund. Technology stocks collapsed months later and still haven't fully recovered since those crazy days. There is no such thing as a "New Economy" or any other tagline or buzzword people may use to suggest that somehow the laws of nature have been repealed. It's never going to be "different this time."

Other People's Money

One of the most important things I've ever learned about how money works is that I could do what the big guys do—use other people's money to make money. That's what I did in the 1970s when I realized I could borrow against my home value and invest the bank's money at a much higher return in John Templeton's mutual fund.

One of the benefits of using a mortgage to obtain investment funds is that some investors may be able to deduct the interest cost. If all those people who borrowed against their homes during the housing bubble had invested that money instead of buying second homes and expensive toys, there would be a lot more wealthy people in the country.

The same mechanics are at work for those who, thinking they were avoiding risk, put all their spare cash into paying off their mortgages. A paid-off home is a part of an asset class (land, real estate) that, over long periods of time, has averaged inflation-like returns, and is subject to both upside and downside risk. The downside is you can't sell off a few square feet of your home to raise money. And unless you live in a state with no property tax, you'll never really own your house. You'll just lease it from the state until you sell it.

If you take the equity out of your home instead and invest it in a diversified ownership portfolio, you can get to that money anytime you choose, including during a crisis if you need extra money to live and pay your mortgage.

Paying down your mortgage might make you feel good but it robs you of wealth-building opportunities. A home should not be seen as an investment asset. It is a necessary cost—you have to live somewhere and pay somebody for the right to do so. Instead of paying the bank, why not pay yourself?

Using a home equity loan as investment capital you'll be making money on other people's money. That's how banks make money—they take your deposits and CDs and then they lend it out at a higher interest rate.

How much to borrow? In most cases I advise responsible clients to borrow up to 80 percent of the home's value and invest it in a diversified ownership portfolio hedged for safety, and let it grow. At certain opportune times, I advise them to take a second mortgage on the remaining 20 percent, such as during the market collapse of 2001-2002.

Investors can also use other people's money in an investment account that offers margin, which is the Wall Street term for the right to borrow against assets in a brokerage account. Margin is handy because it's the same as cash, and if used correctly, you can take advantage of bargains. And, unlike a mortgage, you don't have to make regular interest payments. The interest is added to the loan balance.

A good example of how to use margin wisely is the case of a retired client who wanted to buy a car and wanted to take $35,000 out of her account to pay for it. I didn't think it was a good time for her to sell because the market was low and she would get socked with a tax bill. I did some research and discovered that she could lease the car for $500 a month and showed her that we could make the lease payments by borrowing against her brokerage account, so it wouldn't have any effect on her monthly expenses, and she wouldn't lose out on a future increase in her investments.

She leased the car for two years. In those two years her investment portfolio did extremely well and when the lease was up, she had a big-enough profit that allowed her to cover her margin and leasing expenses, and she got to drive a new car for two years for free!

Margin has a bad reputation with some people because it is widely used by short-term speculators. It was margin debt that aggravated the Crash of 1929 and the mechanics were much the same as the subprime mortgage disaster of 2007. Too many people were speculating with other people's money. But margin has its place in a portfolio, so long as you know what you're doing and you're not using it for short term speculation.

When the Iron's Hot

A great time to utilize leverage is during those periodic spasms of financial crisis when the mob is busy jumping off the cliff and prices are plunging farther than they should. I've done this seventeen times since the fall of 1977. I'm listing some of them here to give you a sense of how to tell when the iron's hot and it's time to strike.

Historical Moments When the Market Was On Sale

1977: In the second half of the year the market dropped 20 percent and I was sure it wasn't the end of the world. I had discovered John Templeton's mutual fund, so I mortgaged the house and invested the money. The house was worth about $25,000. My initial loan was $7000.

1978: The stock market again fell 20 percent and again I invested more.

1979: Fed Chairman Paul Volcker gave a speech in October promising to slow inflation in the money supply. The market sank. All the other

Fed chairmen had lied so I didn't believe him. I margined and bought some more.

1982: This, in retrospect, was the Big Kahuna, the very bottom of the stock market (in August) and the beginning of the trend of the past quarter century. Everyone was badmouthing the economy but anyone could see that stock prices were ridiculously cheap by any measure. That was the first time I sent out a newsletter telling clients now is the time to borrow and buy.

1984: After a good run, and in December, after a good correction, all the "experts" were saying the market was over-extended and couldn't sustain its level, and would again drop to below 1000. I borrowed and bought.

1987: In October, the Dow fell 500 points in one day, the biggest one-day decline in history. Terror was everywhere. So was opportunity. The market rebounded within two years.

1990: The Gulf War. The market sank. The "experts" feared we would be stuck in another quagmire like Vietnam. I'm a pilot and I know you can't hide in the desert, so I was sure it would be a very short war. In October, I sent out a post-card to clients telling them that I was a buyer and suggested they, "Beg, borrow, mortgage your house, your spouse, and buy." Three years later, the accounts who margined had tripled, and we sold enough to pay off the debts.

1995–1996: Another short-term panic that allowed us to buy more at bargain prices.

1998: A worldwide currency crisis hit the stock market that fall as a major hedge fund, Long Term Capital, collapsed. I again urged my clients to borrow and buy, and then we sold enough eight months later to cover the debt. We took the profits in the spring of 1999, less than a year before the bubble burst.

2001: The volatility in the aftermath of the terrorist attacks in September, and the start of the war in Afghanistan, provided opportunities to get in cheap while most people were panicking about the future. As horrific as those attacks were, I advised clients to remember that life goes on, people still need housing, and food. The economy slowed for awhile but survived as always and resumed its normal growth.

2008: The mortgage crisis, massive bank write-downs, and fears of a recession caused the market to drop nearly 20 percent in the beginning of the year. I took advantage of the market "sale" and borrowed money to invest in a diversified portfolio of equity mutual funds.

History teaches us that long-term investing is your friend, and the emotions of fear and greed are your enemies. Do not invest money that you might need to live on, or need for some important purpose in the next year or two. That would be speculating, and speculators are people who are driven by fear and greed, and who ultimately lose.

Ignore them and pay attention to history.

PART III:

Putting It All Together

8

Insurance Simplified

> **Insurance: An ingenious modern game of chance in which the player is permitted to enjoy the comfortable conviction that he is beating the man who keeps the table.**
>
> —*Ambrose Bierce, author*

THERE ARE good reasons to carry insurance and an unlimited number of permutations in the kinds you can buy. It is one of the most misunderstood transactions, so I am including on the following pages a brief primer on some essential forms and how you can get the best value for your money.

Insurance salesmen have been known to push certain types of insurance because they earn a higher commission, as I learned early in my career (see the story in the introduction). There is no one-size-fits-all, and the purchase of insurance should be considered as part of your overall financial plan.

Also, many people make the mistake of buying insurance and forgetting about it when, in reality, insurance needs will change over time. You may be spending money on premiums for coverage you no longer need.

Disability Insurance

Ask your insurance agent or, if you work for a company that provides it, go to your human resources department and ask three questions.

○ What percent of your income does the insurance coverage replace?
○ How long must you be disabled before the benefits begin?
○ Once the benefits begin, how long do they last?

If your benefits only last six months, then you only have short-term disability and will need another policy to fill in.

You should question whether you even need disability insurance. If you are under 55 years old, you are more likely to become disabled than to die. If you are over 55, you will be more likely to die than become disabled.

Check the annual social security statement you receive in the mail to see how much you will be entitled to should you become disabled. Once you know this figure, you can fill in the deficit by buying more if needed.

Something else to keep in mind: if your employer pays your premiums, any benefits you receive will be taxable. However, if you pay the premiums, the benefits will not be taxable. This can add up to serious money.

Mortgage Insurance

Avoid it. It is designed so that if you die, the insurance company pays off your mortgage, relieving your heirs of that expense. The problem is that mortgage insurance is expensive and could have tax consequences for your heirs when you die.

A better idea is to carry enough life insurance (which is cheaper) to provide your spouse a monthly income that is equal to the mortgage payment plus additional income to maintain the surviving spouse's standard of living. Remember that mortgage interest is tax deductible so keeping the mortgage could be beneficial to your heirs.

Homeowner Insurance

If you have a mortgage on your house, coverage is required depending on how much equity you have, to protect the lender. Too many people have coverage that exceeds the market value of the house.

You should first determine the appraised value of your house to see if you're carrying too much coverage. Then, take a closer look to see how much of this value is in the land.

It may be that a $300,000 property is really a $255,000 house on a $45,000 lot. Does it make sense to insure your grass? If not, you should reduce your coverage to match the replacement cost of the building(s).

Most people never review this coverage because it is usually paid as part of your mortgage payment and the mortgage company pays it to the insurer. A lot of people are over-insured and do not realize it. I advise clients in this situation to reduce their coverage and increase the deductible to where they are comfortable.

Auto Insurance

If you are a parent with teenaged children who are driving an older car with no liens against it, the cost of insuring the car itself is probably more than what you'd ever get from the insurance company if the car were destroyed. At least raise your deductible to your comfort level.

If you keep a car a long time, the car comes down in value and at some point you no longer need as much coverage for the same reason—you'll never get from the insurance company enough to compensate for the cost of the premium.

Also, keep up to date on the lowest quotes. As you age, assuming you maintain a good driving record, your premiums should be steadily declining. Shop around and make sure you're getting the best deal.

Medical Insurance

People tend to believe that the cheapest medical insurance they can get is through work, but this is not always so. The older you are, the more pre-existing conditions you have, the more likely that it is cheaper to get coverage through work.

If you are younger with no pre-existing conditions, you might be better off to be on your own plan. Most people take whatever their company offers but if you are smart, you'll shop around.

If a high number of people in your company get cancer and you are on a group plan, your rate will go up. In that case, you might do better on your own. Your employer may not allow you to abandon their plan for your own but you really ought to check it out. You may have no need for drug abuse or maternity coverage but on a group plan you are included for those risks and are paying higher premiums as a result. Keep you eyes open for cheaper alternatives.

Long Term Care Insurance

Long term care (LTC) insurance is no different from other types of insurance. The people selling it play on your emotions. What they do not tell you is that there are five ways to pay for it. I am not opposed to LTC insurance, but urge you to check out all the options.

They include Medicare, Medicaid, having a relative who is able to pay for it, or paying for it yourself. Most people do not know about Medicare and Medicaid. Speak with an expert who can understand these options.

LTC insurance is most valuable to investors who could lose it all if they become sick and need extended, expensive care. In today's dollars, if you retire with a $1 million portfolio and you are withdrawing 6 percent a year, you're receiving $60,000 annually plus another $15,000 or so in Social Security. You may also have a pension on top of that. That amount should cover you if you need long term care, so you don't need the insurance.

At $500,000 or less in a portfolio, you should consider LTC insurance, especially if you want to leave money to your children.

It's important to weigh the cost of this insurance against the opportunity for growth if that money was left in your investment portfolio. It's really a personal choice as to what gives you the most peace of mind.

If you do get a LTC policy, make sure you get one with inflation protection on it. If you are unsure what to do, you can get a policy that covers a portion of your care costs.

In any case, do not be swayed by a salesman's argument based on statistics. You are not a statistic, and statistics can be manipulated to support any argument.

Life Insurance

If you have dependents and you are not yet financially independent, you need life insurance to cover the difference between what you have already acquired and what would be needed if you were not here to provide.

As your living estate increases, you can reduce your coverage as long as your dependents' requirements have not increased. This allows you to reduce the unnecessary premiums and put those dollars to work in your investment portfolio.

Your long-term financial goal should always be to acquire a living estate (financial independence), thus eliminating the need for a death estate (life insurance). Since life insurance premiums are an expense you pay with after-tax dollars, you will want to eliminate this expense as soon as possible.

One of the common mistakes people make is carrying life insurance when they have no dependents to protect. Another is the example I used early in this book, paying extra premiums for life insurance against the death of a minor child. Unless your child is a movie star or actor or musical prodigy whose income is supporting the family, you don't need to spend that money on premiums. Insure your assets, not your liabilities.

If you are single and nobody depends on your income except you, you don't need life insurance. If you are married and both you and your spouse work outside the home and either of your incomes could pay the bills, you don't need life insurance.

If you do need life insurance, term insurance is likely going to be your best option. It is the cheapest way to get the coverage you need. Insurance agents will try to sell you on the "value" of other policies such as whole life, universal life, and variable universal life. But the value is in higher commissions for the agent. In reality, all life insurance is term insurance.

Life insurance is sometimes a necessity but always a poor investment. Don't believe insurance salespeople who tell you otherwise.

Making Good Choices

In general, many people buy either too much insurance or not enough. Both can be costly mistakes. If you buy too little, you may be leaving yourself and your heirs without a safety net. If you buy too much, you'll be laying out money for premiums that could be earning you money in an investment portfolio.

You should be regularly reviewing your insurance coverage and policies as part of your financial plan. Look at deductibles to make sure you aren't paying for coverage that you could handle on your own. If you feel comfortable increasing deductibles, you'll be freeing up cash to add to your investment portfolio.

If your wealth has grown, you may find that you are in a position to insure yourself.

You should always be looking for opportunities to maximize your cash flow so that every dollar possible is working for you and not for the insurance company.

The Annuity Shell Game

ONE OF THE fastest-growing areas of insurance is annuities and it is also one of the worst places anyone could ever put their money. Most investors should never have an annuity.

Annuities are what you get when you combine insurance and investing, and the key selling point is that the taxes are deferred. Regardless of the tax deferral, if you are serious about building and maintaining wealth, you should keep these two functions—insurance and investing—separate.

Insurance companies want a piece of your investment pie and the way they get it is by selling you on the emotional "security" and "logic" in buying their annuities.

The definition of an annuity is a series of equal pay-

I could make more money selling annuities because annuity salespeople earn huge commissions, but it would be at the expense of my clients.

ments. It is a product sold by insurance companies, and many are designed to look like a mutual fund wrapped up inside an insurance product.

As a licensed securities and insurance representative, I receive all the sales material from the insurance companies wanting me to sell their annuities to the public. If annuities were truly designed to help people build and maintain wealth, I would consider recommending them because the way I make money is when I help my clients make money.

I could make a lot more money selling annuities because annuity salespeople earn huge commissions, but it would be at the expense of my clients. Annuities are often sold by individuals who market themselves as a "Senior Specialist" or a "Retirement Specialist." These folks earn as much as 15 percent of your money from commissions. They are doing what they have been told to do, and most are ignorant about how to build wealth. Most of the time, they just don't know any better and that's just fine with the companies that sell annuities. That way, the sales people have no guilt, which they would if they knew the truth.

You may have received an invitation to an annuity sales presentation. The insurance companies offer these all the time and they are usually elaborate and include a free dinner at a fancy restaurant. Some will ask you to bring your brokerage statements with you. That way, they can see exactly how much you have to invest and more effectively convince you to switch to their annuities.

Annuities are sold as an investment product that creates protection from taxes. Uninformed investors are typically more focused on what things cost rather than what they can earn, so these investors are quick to believe that tax protection is a good deal. But it is far more complicated than that, and the downside is huge.

The "good" old days, as promoted by the annuity industry in the 1960s

"**How we retired in 15 years with $300 a month**"

"Look at us! We're retired and having the time of our lives. A fish story? It sure isn't! Let me tell you about it.

"I started thinking about retiring in 1950. Nancy thought I was silly. It all seemed so far away. 'And besides,' she said, 'it makes me feel old.' It didn't seem silly to me, though. We'd just spent the afternoon with Nancy's aunt and uncle. Uncle Will had turned 65 during the war, and, by 1945, his working days were over.

"Now, life seemed to be standing still for them. They couldn't take even the short weekend trips that their friends could easily afford; they couldn't visit their children as often as they'd like.

"A pretty grim existence, I thought. But why? He'd had a good job. Then Nancy reminded me . . . they'd never planned ahead. During her uncle's working years, his paycheck was spent almost as soon as it arrived.

"Fortunately, they had put some money aside for a rainy day. But they hadn't planned ahead enough to make those retirement days sunny!

"I showed Nancy a ▓▓▓▓▓ advertisement I'd seen in Life magazine a week or so before. It described their retirement income plan, telling how a man of 40 could retire in 15 years with a guaranteed income of $300 or more for life!

"Nancy agreed it was a great idea. The thought of retiring at 55 didn't make her feel old at all! So I filled out the coupon that day and sent it right off.

This story is typical. Assuming you start early enough, you can plan to have an income of from $50 to $300 a month or more—beginning at age 55, 60, 65 or older. Send the coupon and receive by mail, without charge or obligation, a booklet which tells about ▓▓▓▓▓ Plans. Similar plans are available for women—and for Employee Pension Programs. Send for your free copy now. In 15 years you'll be glad you did!

Vol. 60, No. 3
January 21 1966

Types of Annuities

Fixed Annuities:

These work much like a bank certificate of deposit, guaranteeing an annual fixed percentage return over a set period of time. Once the period expires, the return is set by the insurance company based on the going rate in the market at the time. Insurance companies entice prospective investors by promising a minimum rate.

The problem starts when you need the money for an emergency and you are slapped with a "surrender" fee: a penalty you pay for canceling the fixed annuity contract. These vary but in many cases exceed 10 percent.

The money you put into a fixed annuity goes into a big pot that has all the insurance company's assets. If the insurance company goes bankrupt, you can lose your money. Informed investors avoid exposure to other people's creditors, so there is hardly a reason to own a fixed annuity.

Finally, if there is ever a monetary crisis and the currency collapses, you will lose because these annuities are claims on paper money.

Immediate Annuities:

Similar to fixed annuities, as the name suggests you start receiving payments immediately after giving the insurance company your money and continue to for the rest of your life. Some companies offer immediate annuities that continue making payments to your spouse after you die.

The notion of "income for life" sounds good. But when you factor in the ravages of inflation, it's another story. The fixed dollar amount that the insurance company promises to pay will buy you less and less of what you need as the years pass. Safety is the preservation of your buying power, so an annuity that pays a fixed dollar amount would be a poor investment decision.

Variable Annuities:

These are like a mutual fund wrapped inside an insurance product. Your money goes into accounts that look like mutual funds, will not be exposed to creditors of the insurance company, is actually invested in something, and includes a death benefit.

The money grows tax-deferred until you take it out, after age 59 1/2 without penalty. The downside is that when you take the money out, the gains are taxed at ordinary income tax rates. If you had instead invested this same money in a mutual fund and you took the money out, you would be taxed at the capital gains rate, currently a maximum of 15 percent.

So if you have such an annuity, you are deferring 15 percent over time so that you can pay ordinary income tax, up to 35 percent on federal income presently, when you withdraw. In higher tax brackets, with state taxes included, the bite gets close to 50 percent.

In 2008, if you are in the lower two income

tax brackets, your capital gains rate goes to zero. So you wouldn't want to buy an annuity because if you pull the money out after 2008, you will pay ordinary income tax rates. If you choose a mutual fund and pull the money out after 2008, you will pay capital gains rates which, for those in the lower tax brackets, could be nothing.

Equity Indexed Annuities:

You may have seen advertisements for equity indexed annuities (EIA) that declare: "S&P 500 Returns—No Risk." EIAs guarantee your principal and offer you participation in the stock market. These are actually fixed annuities dressed up with fancy features. The benefit to the companies selling them is that anyone with a simple insurance license, as opposed to a brokers license, can sell them.

The insurance company invests your money by placing the majority of it in investment grade bonds to guarantee your principal. After paying the sales person's commissions, the rest goes into stock market options, which are a way to bet on the market without actually owning stocks.

In a low interest rate environment, where we are at this writing, it takes a lot more of your premium to purchase the investment grade bonds because as interest rates fall the price of bonds rise. That leaves only a small amount left over to play the stock market.

Also, there is a limit on what you earn regardless of what the stock market does. Most are capped somewhere between 7 and 10 percent. You could have bought an EIA in 2003 capped at 7 percent that was tied to the Dow Jones Industrial Average, which rose 22 percent that year.

But when you get your statement, you only received 4.7 percent. Why? Because interest rates were low and it took a lot more of your premium to cover the bond purchase, leaving only a small amount left over for the stock market.

"That variable annuities hold more than $1 trillion in assets is a testament to the powerful incentives created by the insurance industry with generous commissions and the massive fraud they engender."

EIAs are incredibly complex products which are poorly understood by most of the people selling them, and full of loopholes that hurt the buyers. A number of research papers have recently been published that declare them one of the most fraudulent products sold to investors today.

Annuities Versus Mutual Funds

To illustrate the difference between annuities and mutual funds, let's invest a hypothetical $100,000 in a stock mutual fund and the same amount in a variable annuity which invests in a stock mutual fund. The annuity salesperson will argue that the variable annuity is better because it grows tax-deferred, whereas you have to pay taxes on the mutual fund as it grows.

But you aren't getting the whole story. Suppose these two investments both double. Each is now worth $200,000. You are so overcome with joy you have a heart attack and die.

Your spouse calls up the investment advisor asking how much each of your accounts are worth. Each account is now worth $200,000. Your spouse decides to buy another house and wants to cash out one of those investments.

If he or she sells the variable annuity, taxes could take as much as 35 percent.

If the mutual fund is sold instead, the tax is based on the gain after your death, which could be nothing, and even if there is a gain after your death, the tax rate is at the capital gains rate. So the supposed benefit of the tax-deferred variable annuity is virtually nonexistent over the long-term.

But don't just take my word for it. In a 2005 research paper, Dr. Craig McCann and Kaye Thomas of the Securities Litigation and Consulting Group, stated:

> "Annuities stand out as the investment most likely to be unsuitable since in virtually every instance, the investor would have been better served by [a] mutual fund or a portfolio of individual stocks. That variable annuities hold more than $1 trillion in assets is a testament to

the powerful incentives created by the insurance industry with generous commissions and the massive fraud they engender."

The Annuity Flipper Scam

The majority of annuity sales are to people who already own an annuity. This is known as annuity "flipping." The only way to get out of an annuity without the tax consequences is typically to buy a new annuity in what is called a 1035 exchange, named for the IRS rule that covers it.

The sales pitch goes something like this: "You need to change your annuity you have now with Company X and we need to move it over to this new annuity with Company Y because if you want to get all the new features that are available, like in a new car, you need to upgrade every couple of years."

The real purpose is that the sales person gets a new commission if they can get you to switch companies.

If you still believe that an annuity is a good investment, consider the Deficit Reduction Act passed by the federal government. Under this new law, in many cases if you apply for Medicaid, you have to change the beneficiary of your annuity from your loved ones to the state government so the government gets its money back.

What To Do If You Already Own An Annuity

If you got this book too late and want to get out of an annuity, what you can do depends on your situation because there is so much variation in all the annuity contracts out there. Some annuity contracts are hundreds of pages long. Even the people who sell them often have no idea what the details are.

If you have an annuity and it has grown, it might cost you serious money in taxes to surrender it. You may have to pay a penalty if you take it out before 59 1/2.

Many people get stuck in annuities and there is little they can do about it. Unfortunately, sometimes the best option is to do a 1035 exchange to get into a different annuity that has better investment options with lower fees.

If you have been sold an annuity and it costs too much in taxes and penalties to get out, one option is to write it off as a loss on your income tax return. In this case, it might be possible to get out of the annuity and not pay taxes at all.

Another option is to annuitize the annuity. This sounds confusing but it means taking your lump sum annuity and make it into a series of payments. There are a lot of options available to you with this choice. For example, you could opt for a life annuity that will pay you a certain amount of dollars per month for life or for a certain period of time that would include your heirs if you should die before the time is up.

The benefits of this are that each payment is part principal and part gain, so it helps to spread out your tax liability. Also, the surrender charge can be eliminated. Before annuitizing, you must review your annuity contract because they are all different.

The income you receive by annuitizing the annuity can be used to supplement your retirement needs or you can invest this money in a better way. This allows you to pass the money to your heirs at your time of death on a stepped-up basis (they will only pay tax on any increase that takes place after your death). You also benefit by only having to pay capital gains rates rather than ordinary income tax rates.

If you've put retirement money into an annuity (known as a qualified annuity), getting the money out is easier because you don't have to worry about the tax liability. The only thing you need to worry about is the surrender charge.

If you are okay with paying the surrender charge, you can transfer to another retirement investment vehicle and be done with the annuity.

The Case For Common Sense

As an investment advisor, my job is protect people who trust me from making bad choices. But all too often, I don't get the chance. New and existing clients will come to me after some other company has talked them into buying an annuity, and ask me what it is and how it works.

The person who sold it to them (who made a generous commission doing so) may have explained it, but even if they did, odds are what they said was inaccurate, incomplete, or downright misleading. And the customer wasn't listening. When a product's prospectus can be upwards of 400 pages long, how could anyone understand it? When I try to help them by calling the company, even the people at the other end of the line don't understand them.

What causes common sense to fly out the window? Why do so many people allow themselves to be talked into making important decisions without knowing the implications?

From my side of the desk, it's clear that the time, discipline, and knowledge of the wealth building process required for success is almost too much for the average person to take on. That's why I'm always in favor of hiring an independent advisor who has no conflicts of interest.

When shopping for an investment advisor, look for:

○ Enough experience to have gone through a variety of market ups and down.

○ Independence from any major banks, brokerage firms, or insurance companies that will want them to push their employers' products.

○ Someone who invests their money the same way they would invest yours, and can show you how they've done. Most advisors make their money selling you something, not by being successful investors.

○ Someone who takes the time to educate and advise you, rather than trying to sell you something.

○ Someone who is willing to continue educating you whether or not you invest with them. I do this through my radio show, seminar series, and online.

○ Someone who exhibits an understanding of the big picture and the long term, and who is focused on helping you fashion your investments to support your personal goals.

Long-Haul Retirement

THE THREE principal enemies of money are fear, taxes, and inflation. Fear and taxes can be controlled to some degree. Inflation is the hidden, constant thief of your money, and it is especially dangerous to those who retire without having taken it into account in all their financial choices.

The days when people died within ten years of retirement are long gone. People are retiring earlier, they are going to live many years longer and healthier than earlier generations, and many will wake up one day to discover that they have outlived their money.

This already is happening. We know of an elderly woman whose wealthy husband died in the early 1980s at a time when plain bank CDs were yielding as much as 12 percent, which sounds like a lot but in fact was actually a net loss because inflation and taxes were extremely high. Nevertheless, they were enjoying the best of everything, and the dying husband kept telling his wife, "Honey, just keep rolling the CDs over and you'll be fine. Don't let anyone talk you into doing anything else. Just keep rolling them over."

The widow did just that. Interest rates began to decline and so did her income. But she kept on living as she had, dipping into principal. After 15 years of this, she was living on Social Security in a trailer park, wondering where the money went.

I faced this issue on my parents' behalf many years ago when I got started in my business. It was the defining moment in my full understanding of how to make money work as hard and as smart as it can. I wanted to know how I could set up my mother and father with retirement income that would be protected against inflation. I knew that anything tied to paper money was a bad bet, and that if my parents invested conventionally they'd probably outlive their income.

As I've mentioned, the investment industry wants you to believe that as you age you should reduce the amount of money you have in the stock market and increase what you have in bonds. That's the ridiculous advice you often hear: subtract your age from 100 to get the percentage of your portfolio that should be in stocks: at age 60 you should be 40 percent in stocks, 60 percent in bonds. Whoever thought this formula up was probably an investment person trying to sell something.

The investment industry wants you to believe that as you age you should reduce the amount of money you have in the stock market.

I hope I have successfully debunked that idea but in case you have any doubts, consider that historically bonds significantly lag stocks, and they are tied to the value of a depreciating paper currency. Look at the chart on Page 87 and you'll see what I mean.

MORE SECURITY FOR THE AMERICAN FAMILY

THE SOCIAL SECURITY ACT AS AMENDED OFFERS GREATER OLD-AGE INSURANCE PROTECTION TO PEOPLE NOW NEARING RETIREMENT AGE.

Your Money Doesn't Know How Old You Are

It is good to have something to rely on. For now, we have Social Security, which is raised each year to reflect the rate of inflation. Many people also have pensions from civil service or other employment, usually without inflation protection.

But parking an ever-increasing share of your wealth in interest-paying bonds violates one of the basic rules of investing: always aim to be an owner. When you "buy" a bond, you are lending money and getting an IOU with income, instead of being an owner sharing in profits, as you are when you buy stock.

The IOU of a bond is guaranteed, but not the income. That means there are times when interest rates fall so low, as they did in 2008, that bonds pay less than the rate of inflation, so bondholders are actually losing buying power.

All your core investments should be as a true owner. So I advise clients to put that same retirement money into diversified mutual funds that invest in the stock market, and take out up to 5 percent a year. If they can take out less, so much the better. But up to 5 percent is safe enough to be certain that you don't dip into your principal over the long run.

It's also a good idea to keep a couple of years of living expenses in a liquid account, so you know you can weather a bad patch in the market and still meet an emergency. Beyond that, if you see yourself living awhile longer, perhaps are inclined to leave a legacy fund for heirs, and if you or your investment advisor did a good job of diversifying your investments, there's no reason to change your approach as you go into retirement.

> **Your money doesn't know how old you are, so you should think of yourself as an investor until the day you die.**

Your money doesn't know how old you are, so you should think of yourself as an investor until the day you die. If you made good choices during the years of accumulation, you should just keep doing it that way when you retire.

Common sense, as I've described it in these pages, is common sense at any age. If you don't pay too much for things, manage your taxes, diversify, and stay disciplined, it doesn't matter if you're 21 or 81—when opportunity comes along it makes sense to take advantage of it.

Why Not Grow Rich While Growing Old?

The wealth-building power of long-term stock owner-ship is sometimes staggering. Among the stories we know of is the son of a 35-year United Parcel Service driver who died just as the company was going public, and discovered he had inher-ited a modest ranch house and $100 million in UPS stock.

In spite of the rise and fall of the economy over the years, the number of millionaires in the U.S. has continued to grow. Most recent estimates put it at three million, or just under one in a hundred.

Many of those millionaires got there by investing for the long term. If in 1976 you put $100,000 into John Templeton's fund, and then withdrew 5 percent at the end of each year for 30 years, your first year you would taken out $4,500 (after expenses), but because it was a good year in the market, you would have ended up with $120,000. If you left it there and kept taking out 5 percent a year for 30 years, your principal would have grown to $1.3 million and your 5 percent annual withdrawal would be up to $63,000.

Everything costs more today than it did 30 years ago, but your mutual fund investment would have beaten inflation by a wide margin. So while you were receiving income, as you grew older you would also have been growing wealthier.

If instead you had put that same amount of money in municipal bonds, for example, your income would have stayed the same, being eroded by inflation.

Harder Than It Needs To Be

One of the most difficult questions people face when contemplating the third act of their lives is, How much is enough? What amount of money constitutes financial independence?

The answer, of course, is that it depends. One of the things it depends on is your relationship with money. There are more people than you might imagine who have $10 million at their disposal but shop in thrift stores because they are afraid they'll outlive their money.

On the other hand, a New York estate lawyer we know of tells the story of a client who'd just sold his share of a business for $600 million and declared that, rather than retire, "I want to see if I can make some *real* money."

A very small percentage of Americans—perhaps two or three out of a hundred—ever achieve true financial independence. About half of them inherited or married their wealth. Of the remaining ones who built wealth on their own, half of those did it through ownership of a business. The rest have done it though successful, long-term investing.

> **I have yet to meet a wealthy person who became financially independent through speculation, but I know a lot of speculators who made it big and, sooner or later, lost it.**

Clients who achieved financial independence the gradual way have included all sorts of middle-class workers from school teachers to iron workers. I'm convinced that any young person today can become financially independent if they follow the basic rules. But it takes patience and time.

Where people get into trouble is when they become impatient and want to speed up the wealth creation process. But trying to speed up the clock means taking bigger risks, becoming a speculator instead of an investor. I have yet to meet a wealthy person that became financially independent through speculation, but I know a lot of speculators who made it big and, sooner or later, lost it. Speculation is like an addiction. Once you're hooked, it's hard to go back to basics.

Retirement Spending

Retire is probably a word we shouldn't use anymore because so few people will be able to and the rest don't want to. We need to invent a new term to describe the post-career years. But one thing won't change: you need money to live at any age and how much money you'll have and how long it lasts depends on how you spend it.

It's typical that people spend more in the first few years after they stop working. But disciplined savers often need encouragement. Their portfolio continues to grow and their income exceeds what they made while working. They are stuck in the saving mode and I finally tell them that if they don't start spending, their children will do it for them.

In spite of the conversations I have with clients about being prepared for the bad year or two, some just don't want to adapt their spending. During the bad couple of years that followed 2000, for example, I had a few clients who kept on spending the same number of dollars even though their portfolios were smaller due to the decline in the market.

As a result, they were spending more than the 5 percent I recommend of the total portfolio and, after some time, had to dig into principal. Those who followed my advice to keep a few years expenses in a separate fixed income account ended up in good shape.

A Final Thought

Nothing I've discussed here is new, revolutionary, or odd. It's all based on common sense and logic. Little of what I've discussed will you learn from most sales people in the investment industry because they don't understand it, or they can't make as much money recommending it.

If you decide to manage your own investments, you now know the basics of success. Whether you are a success will depend on how well you follow the guidelines, and how well you are able to keep your emotions under control.

If you decide to give your money to an investment advisor, there are two tests of whether you should trust them with your money. First, I recommend you give that person a copy of this book and ask them to read it and let you know if they agree with the concepts and tactics. If they don't, I suggest you move on.

The second and perhaps most important test is to ask your investment advisor if their own money is invested in the same way as their clients. My money is invested exactly like my clients, side-by-side.

You have a right and an obligation to ask these questions and a responsibility to yourself to be guided by the answers.

And speaking of answers, I don't claim to have them all. In these pages I have described how I learned what I know and how I've put it to work for myself and my clients. If you know a better way, I'd like to hear about it. Although there is no perfect plan, I'll never stop trying to perfect the plan I have.

My hope is that I have given you enough answers so that you can ask good questions. Money is dynamic, and the world is always changing, so the answers will change as well.

If you're curious to know more and want to keep up with the latest developments, visit my blog: ManarinOnMoney.com, or email me: investor@manarin.com.

Until then, stay disciplined, remain diversified, and be an owner!

Peace and goodwill,

Roland Manarin

Acknowledgements

To Don Davidson, for twisting my arm and convincing me to make this book happen. Thank you!

To Foster Winans, for sharing your talents as a creative editor and literary artist. Thank you!

To "Professor" Tim Bastian for your contributions to Chapter 9 on annuities. Thank you!

To my family, children, and friends. Thank you!

To my staff at Manarin Investment Counsel. Thank you!

To the individuals, families, and businesses that make up my community of clients. Thank you!

And to you, the reader. Thank you!

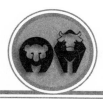

About the Author

Roland R. Manarin arrived in America in 1954 as a ten-year-old immigrant, in a European family of marble workers that had survived the economic and political upheavals of World War II and after, in Breslau, Germany and later in northern Italy. His father had been recruited by an American contractor to move to Omaha, Nebraska. Once he had saved enough money, his father brought over the rest of the family, including  Roland, who quickly learned English and worked from junior high through college as a clerk in a grocery store.

What saved the Manarins from ruin in Europe was the small nest egg of gold his father had managed to accumulate before the Germans and then the Soviets made it difficult to make a steady living. Roland grew up keenly aware of the preciousness of money, and curious about how it works.

After a stint selling life insurance, then office equipment and business forms, he was talked by a friend into becoming a stock broker for a large firm. He rose through the ranks to become one of the firm's top brokers, until his superiors pressured him to sell his clients inappropriate investments because they would earn him a bigger commission.

He quit and started his own company. A quarter century later, Manarin Investment Counsel, Ltd., is an independent registered investment advisory firm with headquarters in Omaha, Nebraska, managing assets of more than $500 million. *Barron's* magazine has twice singled Roland out for recognition, as one of "America's Best Wealth Advisors" in 2004, and one of the "Top 100 Independent Financial Advisers" in 2007.

Inspired by the example of the legendary investor John Templeton, he launched the Lifetime Achievement Fund, a globally diversified, professionally-managed public mutual fund in which he keeps the lion's share of his own wealth.

For three decades he has been on a mission to educate people about the common mistakes made around money, teaching a free, three-part monthly seminar series on personal finance, economics, and the investment markets. His weekly radio show, "It's Your Money," has been on the air for more than two decades.

Roland lives in Omaha.